Ian Buxton

101 Legendary Whiskies You're Dying to Try
But (Possibly) Never Will

Ian Buxton

101 Legendary Whiskies You're Dying to Try
But (Possibly) Never Will

hachette
SCOTLAND

Copyright © Ian Buxton 2014

The right of Ian Buxton to be identified as the Author of
the Work has been asserted by him in accordance with the
Copyright, Designs and Patents Act 1988.

First published in 2014
by HACHETTE SCOTLAND, an imprint of HACHETTE UK
1

Cataloguing in Publication Data is available from the British
Library

978 1 4722 1067 8

Designed by Lynn Murdie

Printed and bound in China by Imago

Hachette Scotland's policy is to use papers that are natural,
renewable and recyclable products and made from wood
grown in sustainable forests. The logging and manufacturing
processes are expected to conform to the environmental
regulations of the country of origin.

HACHETTE SCOTLAND
An Hachette UK Company
338 Euston Road
London NW1 3BH

www.headline.co.uk
www.hachette.co.uk

Contents

Introduction

What did the whisky that sank with the SS *Politician* in the Outer Hebrides in 1941 (the inspiration for the classic *Whisky Galore!* novel and film) really taste like? I suppose we could still find some antique islander who might, suitably refreshed, recall its clandestine and furtive tang. Perhaps a fugitive bottle might emerge from deep in Eriskay's machair or the peat bogs of Barra (there were 264,000 bottles on board, after all). But perhaps it's better that it remains elusive and indescribable. It is a legendary whisky after all.

What about the Glenavon Special Liqueur Whisky, so confidently labelled 'Bottled by the Distillers' and, allegedly, the last bottle in existence that sold in November 2006 at Bonham's in London for nearly £15,000? Was it even genuine? Questions were raised at the time but presumably the buyer was happy. After all, with or without provenance, it's a bona fide legend.

History tells us that whisky began its long life in Ireland, where records date it to 1405 (in an obituary for a chieftain who drank himself to death – who says binge drinking is a new problem?), then moved to Scotland where it turns up in the tax records for 1494. (A tax on whisky – who would have guessed?) What did it taste like, then? And is there any way we can actually find out.

A personal blend

Over the years I've slowly built up a list of the whiskies I wish I could drink. It started with 'Lost Legends' – museum-quality, ultra-rare survivors from history that are eagerly sought after by a reclusive, secretive and intensely private group of international collectors. Typically this whisky might be the last-known bottle from a lost distillery (though not every closed distillery is or was legendary – some deserved to close and have been rightly forgotten) or an exceptionally old or very, very valuable, collectable whisky. There are just a few distilleries with a very special place in the hearts of whisky lovers and I've tried to give them due prominence. If ever any of these were seen at auction, a fierce bidding war would ensue, after which the bottle would disappear into a vault or private museum that could be anywhere in the world. It's highly unlikely you'll ever see one of these in the flesh, let alone taste them – this is whisky to dream about!

After that, I took a long look at some of the very, very indulgent bottles that come on the market these days. This is whisky porn – the world's most exclusive and ultra-expensive bottles. They are often more expensive than a perfectly decent family car. And, in a few cases, cost more even than a perfectly decent house. I call these the 'Luxurious Legends' and you can expect to pay anything over a grand for these (I know, I know). Basically you can forget it unless you're a lottery winner, a Premier League footballer or a Russian oligarch. But I have been known to press my nose up against the window of an Aston Martin showroom – it's fun to dream – so I have included them here. And the lottery winner/footballer/oligarch probably feels better about their purchase knowing that you are drooling with envy. Some of these bottles may seem grandiose, vulgar and ostentatious* but they're out there and they aren't going away.

To soften the pain, I began a third list – the 'Living Legends'. Here I catalogue both the whiskies that seem to me under-valued and not fully appreciated and the rare and hard-to-find whiskies from round the world – single-cask bottlings, distillery-only limited editions and collectables. These are generally hard to find, but affordable§ whiskies that are out there somewhere if you are patient and know where to look, and they were all available at the time of writing. You have to move fast for these, though – others are searching as diligently as you, if not harder. In a world of blogging and on-line marketing, such expressions can sell out very fast – sometimes in minutes (I know, it's hard to believe). And they're generally not cheap. Budget at least three figures and, if you have to buy off one of the many on-line auctions that have sprung up, expect to pay a hefty premium. But, unlike my Luxurious Legends, almost any of us might conceivably get to drink one of these whiskies one day without winning the lottery. (Although it might help if one of your Premium Bond numbers comes up.)

And then, as I explored these ideas further, I realised there was an elusive fourth category, that of 'Whisky Legends'. These are the people and distilleries that don't necessarily fit comfortably into any of the first three groups, yet have fascinating stories to tell or which illustrate the cultural hinterland of whisky. The existence of these legends help mark out the cratur from other distilled spirits.

* That's because they are.

§ A relative term in this context, you'll understand.

101 Legendary Whiskies is where the Lost, Luxurious, Living and Whisky Legends meet. Along the way, I share some thoughts on auctions and the curious but increasingly popular habit of collecting whiskies (the distillers love that one) and, at intervals through the text, I include my views on why this all might go wrong and end in tears – feel free to disagree*.

Just for fun, we've mixed them up; presenting them in alphabetical order – hours of fun await you. The categories aren't absolute in any event and the selection is highly personal. In fact, a number of the entries could qualify in more than one category and I'm sure that I will have missed something that you think should be here and included one or two that completely baffle you. But that's the fun of the thing. Just relax: it's only whisky and there are no right or wrong answers, whatever anyone else might try to tell you.

It's been my privilege to sample at least some of the whiskies listed here and to discuss them with the people who make them. It's the least I can do to share that experience. So read on to discover the legendary whiskies you're dying to try but (probably) never will described, discussed, dissected and, in a few cases, drunk (lucky me). But first, age before beauty…

Old is not necessarily good

I once drank an 80-year-old Glenfiddich.

Distilled in 1929, the sample had been drawn in 2009 and was lying in Master Blender David Stewart's§ Tasting Room. (Despite its somewhat unpromising location between Coatbridge and Motherwell, inside what resembles a high-security prison, it's something of an enchanted palace of whiskies.) I pestered him to let me try this nectar and, gracefully, he agreed.

Nineteen twenty-nine was not a great year for Scotch whisky. Hammered by the global economic slump, most of Scotland's distilleries were silent or, if they were very lucky, on short-time working. Presumably Glenfiddich was one of the fortunate ones.

So I approached the glass with a certain nervous apprehension. It's not every day, even in the life of a whisky writer, that you get to try whisky of this antiquity, especially not one from a distillery held in such high esteem as Glenfiddich.

* By the way, there are quite a few footnotes. Read them: some of the best bits are lurking here.
§ Remember David; he's important and we shall meet him again.

After all, this is the distillery that, virtually single-handedly, reminded the world of the virtues of single malt whisky (and, while we're at it, they invented the distillery visitor centre as well) so we've a lot to thank them for. And, even without this heritage, you have to hesitate before downing any 80-year-old spirit.

I'd liken the experience to driving a vintage Bentley – except that after you've driven the Bentley you hand it back and someone else can enjoy its power and incomparable grace. Whereas, once you've drunk the whisky, it's gone and can never be enjoyed again. It's one of the great contradictions of whisky that it only attains its true meaning as it is drunk; something the 'whisky investment' lobby appear unable to understand. Its apotheosis comes at the moment of its obliteration. So the glass I was holding was, quite literally, a vanishing asset and, before swallowing, I had to consider my responsibilities in this matter.

I nosed it very carefully and the aromas were enchanting: it seemed to me that I was inhaling the heady scent of decades. Can one nose in sepia? I sensed vanished hopes and dreams, lost empires and faded glories – though, quite possibly, this owed something to an over-active imagination and an exaggeratedly romantic view of the liquid in my glass. There was the distant memory of the dying embers of a wood fire, some cooked fennel and a fleeting suggestion of sweetness. The colour was fascinating; at the meniscus where liquid and glass seemed eternal partners, there appeared hints of a mossy green colour. Rarely encountered in any spirit, this is suggestive of great age; almost as if ancient liquid lichens have been formed in the glass.

Convinced that it held great mysteries and unexpected depths, I brought it reverently to my lips with an equal measure of trepidation and anticipation. And then spat it out.

'I did warn you,' said David, and indeed he had. The liquid was harsh and bitter, excessively woody and truly unpleasant. It was completely undrinkable: not that Glenfiddich had the slightest intention of selling it. It was a curiosity, kept to satisfy those fortunate few aficionados and connoisseurs who encountered it, and was preserved, I like to imagine, out of a sense of deference and respect for the long-dead distillers who first crafted it.

After all, even if you couldn't use it, you couldn't throw it away any more than you would idly consign a revered ancestor's furniture to the bonfire. And so this whisky lived on as a spectre – its gaunt, skeletal remains forming a liquid memento mori if ever we should forget that some things can live too long.

But it serves a useful purpose here: to remind us that not all old whisky is good, let alone great; that whisky has a finite life (in cask at least) and that it is made to be drunk, not to be worshipped.

Not so very long ago, it was the received and unchallenged wisdom of the Scotch whisky industry that, after 25 years or so in cask, whisky was undrinkable (or, more to the distillers' point, unsaleable); it was overly woody, 'slimy' and well past its best. In recent years, that view has been challenged and overturned. Whiskies of 30 years' vintage are commonplace; a 40-year-old whisky is scarcely to be remarked upon; 50 years remains a landmark but you can encounter drams of greater age without the slightest difficulty.

Indeed, as I write, the oldest Scotch whisky currently for sale is a 70-year-old The Glenlivet from the respected Elgin bottlers Gordon & MacPhail. A few bottles still remain available at around £13,000 each. And that brings up the vexed and hotly debated question of price.

Expensive is not necessarily the best

A Macallan of pensionable age in a Lalique decanter or the 50-year-old Glenfiddich in a hand-blown bottle with a sterling silver label will set you back a few thousand more than the 70-year-old The Glenlivet (who's counting?).

We'd all love to try these whiskies. But there are two problems: first, and most obviously, the price. For that sort of money you could buy a perfectly serviceable car – a brand-spanking-new Ford Focus, for example, and still have change to buy some perfectly fine whisky to toast it. Or you could acquire a seriously nice watch and some extraordinary handmade shoes in the finest crocodile skin. Or a state of the art sound system. You take my point: £13,000 is a lot of money and there is no shortage of lovely things to spend it on.

And it doesn't stop there: as I write, Whyte & Mackay have announced that they've filled some shelves at Harrods with the Richard Paterson Collection of The Dalmore. Twelve bottles for a cool £987,500. Hold me back.

Money can't buy you love – or these bottles

Now we have the second problem: availability. Even if you could afford to buy any of the whiskies in this book you couldn't necessarily get them. Quantities are very limited.

The last bottle of Dalmore Trinitas has gone (at £125,000) but, at the time of writing, you might be lucky and, after due vetting, be allowed to buy one of 60 bottles of Johnnie Walker's Diamond Jubilee for around £100,000 (form an orderly queue, please).

Glenfiddich release only 50 bottles a year of their 50 Year Old; tragically, those Macallan Lalique decanters seem to sell out as soon as they're released; and even obscure Japanese whiskies fetch astronomical prices (Karuizawa 1960, a snip at £12,500).

And, when Whyte & Mackay revealed Dalmore Sirius to an expectant world (distilled in 1951 and thus 58 years old, it was £10,000 – curious how fond the distilling industry is of that magical £10,000 price tag), there were just 12 bottles and they promptly announced that all had been pre-sold!

As they very kindly sent me a tiny phial of Sirius, I'll break off at this point to sample some of that self-same hooch. Wait for it, yes, I can confirm that it's pretty tasty. At a quick calculation I swallowed less than 1cl (1/70th of a bottle). Call it £100 worth, or a great deal more in a bar.

Was it worth it?

Well, that depends. 'Worth' is a relative concept, after all. Clearly there are enough people out there with enough money to find out. Though distillers love the 'gee-whiz' PR to be obtained from these luxury bottles, they aren't offering them and retailers aren't putting them on their shelves just because they look pretty. Believe it or not, they do sell and people do drink them. At least, I hope they drink them.

Great whisky – or just a pretty box?

You do pay a lot for the presentation, however. Lavish packaging has come to dominate these high-end expressions (with some notable exceptions – Glenfarclas comes especially to mind, to their great credit) and it has to be paid for. By the time you add a custom-made crystal decanter, hand-crafted box, leather-bound booklet and special shipping carton, not to mention gimmicks such as fountain pens, silver tasting cups, museum-quality display cases and even archive-quality white gloves to handle the bottle, considerably more than £2,000 can be added to the retail price. After all, everyone wants a bit of the action and with the distiller's, distributor's, wholesaler's and retailer's margin to be covered – not to mention VAT or sales tax – the price soon soars away.

Take the Glenfiddich 50 Year Old, for example. For years it was available in a relatively simple bottle and wooden box for around £5,000, which, you might think, was quite enough for a bottle of whisky. There were only 500 bottles, each packaged in a handmade oak box with a brass plaque; the bottle label and tasting notes personalised with the bottle number and bottling date; and each bottle was signed by Alexander Grant Gordon, former chairman of William Grant & Sons Distillers Ltd and great-grandson of Glenfiddich distillery founder William Grant. To top it off, the happy owner was issued with a certificate and appointed a Freeman of the Glenfiddich Distillery (whatever privileges that may bestow, you have to admit it sounds great).

But then 'Marketing' got their hands on it and it was repackaged and relaunched (generally, when you hear this, check your wallet: it's unlikely to be good news for the humble punter). In July 2009 the 'new' Glenfiddich 50 Year Old was unveiled by Peter Grant Gordon with the claim that 'Glenfiddich 50 Year Old is not just a part of our history; it is our history.'

Was it twice as good as the earlier version? At a staggering £10,000* it was certainly twice as expensive. It came in a hand-blown triangular bottle with a sterling silver label, a leather-bound book of history and tasting notes, a very impressive casket and – of course – the by-now obligatory certificate of authenticity.

I went to meet the chap who blows the bottles. He told me that technically it was extremely demanding to create a triangular bottle at exactly the right size (you wouldn't want your bottle on the small size and you can be sure that Glenfiddich don't want it any larger than it should be) and for every bottle that Glenfiddich accept as perfect, he has eight or nine rejected. Quite right, too, if you're paying that kind of money, but it's a sobering thought when you consider the skill and time that goes into making every one of them. And you can guess who pays for this.

* That was the price at launch. I just checked a well-known website and was even more staggered to see it listed at £15,000.

15

Glenfiddich are not alone (there's a similar story for most of the luxury presentations) but the undeniable fact remains that someone is buying these bottles and the demand for the most outrageously priced whiskies seems to have survived, indeed prospered, during the current economic storms. So we're going to see more of this sort of thing.

I might deplore the trend towards ever more expensive whisky but I can't deny the phenomenon and I wanted to explore what was going on. Yes, it's hard work, but someone has to do it*.

Sadly as they are so rare and obscure, I can't actually tell you what many of these whiskies would cost to buy. Furthermore, prices are changing so fast at the moment that there's a real danger that any I quote would be long out of date by the time this book reaches you. So it seemed pointless to give prices. In any event, the internet does this better. And, for much the same reason, there are no tasting notes. In many cases, I've never tasted the whisky and never will.

Neither will you.

* Very old joke, sorry, but it seemed appropriate.

Luxurious

Producer	Glenmorangie plc
Distillery	Ardbeg, Islay
Visitor Centre	Yes
Availability	Possibly at auction

Ardbeg 1965

40 Years Old

Shortly after this was launched in July 2006, I was accompanying a Russian submarine admiral and his defence contractor 'friend' (guess who was paying) around some distilleries.

'I want one of those Ardbegs in the glass case,' he said. All 261 bottles were sold out but calls were made (I have contacts, I'll have you know) and a bottle was found (guess who paid). In a gesture of thanks he gave me the accompanying mini, which I sold to a Taiwanese collector, some while later, for £650. It seemed an extraordinary amount of money at the time, though I've subsequently been told I could have got £1,000 or more*.

The admiral took his bottle back to Vladivostok and drank it with his chums. We subsequently got him another bottle, but Russian customs impounded it. I wouldn't have messed with him – the guy had nuclear warheads under his control – but apparently they knew better.

At the time, the bottle had been launched at a retail price of £2,000. Writing in the *Scotch Whisky Review*, Dave Broom described it as 'the most absurdly pretentious idea yet from the half-baked minds of luxury whisky marketers.' At the time, I agreed.

And yet... and yet. The fact, unpalatable as I find it, is that it sold out virtually overnight. It sells today for around £6,000 and if they were launching it tomorrow, that would seem cheap. The boom market for this type of trophy whisky seems to have no visible limit. I don't care for the phenomenon but I can't ignore it.

Ardbeg 1965 set – briefly – a new price ceiling and, as such, it qualifies for inclusion here. It wasn't long, though, before other brands stepped in and Ardbeg, determined not to lose out, launched their absurd and ludicrous Double Barrel at £10,000 (as well as two bottles, you got a sort of 'lucky bag' of other very expensive bits and pieces selected apparently at random).

Sooner or later this is going to end badly and someone will get hurt. For the moment, though, price alone has become the signifier and perfectly drinkable whisky gets locked in a vault for cold-hearted Gollums to gloat over.

I could have drunk that mini, I suppose; but what would you have done? I can't imagine it's 'worth' £650. I just hope the guy in Taiwan is happy.

* Collecting mini bottles is strangely addictive it seems. Don't start would be my advice.

2

Producer
Distillery
Visitor Centre
Availability

Glenmorangie plc
Ardbeg, Islay
Yes
Auctions

www.ardbeg.com

Ardbeg Galileo

'As an Ardbeg 10 and Uigeadail fan I tried the Galileo with high anticipation and left feeling they'd made a horrible mistake.'

So wrote 'Islay Peat' on 4th April 2013 on the Whisky.com forum. He wasn't alone. Opinion was violently split on this release from the painfully fashionable Ardbeg. The phrase 'emperor's new clothes' was bandied about. But plenty of people loved it. And then…

And then, *Whisky Magazine* voted it 'World's Best Single Malt Whisky'. Prices soared on internet auction sites, with single bottles fetching as much as £140 (you can get one now for around half that). But permit me to tell you about *my* 'horrible mistake'.

As part of the media briefing, Ardbeg sent out a small number of minis (I've heard fewer than 450) in a metal container like a small cocktail shaker, in a special box. I got one*.

Before I could write about it (*Whisky Advocate* magazine in the USA had commissioned⁵ an article), I foolishly mentioned it to a mini-collecting acquaintance who, before he began frothing at the mouth, begged me to part with it. Numbers were mentioned – scary numbers – resulting in a moral dilemma for your correspondent. So I issued a challenge: get me a bottle and you can have the mini. Remarkably, he pulled it off.

Quandary resolved – Ardbeg got their story; I got more whisky; and that mini survives in a place of honour. All's well, you might think. But then the minis started to pop up on auction sites – the first one sold for £820!

Damn! I could have sold the mini, bought a bottle and trousered £600. That's more – generally a lot more – than I earn for an article. I think that qualifies as a horrible – you could say legendary – mistake, and it is certainly recalled as such in this house.

I have no idea how long this craze for minis, especially those containing peated Islay whisky, will continue. After all, it's not that long since the style was unfashionable – close to unsaleable, even. Blenders only required tiny quantities, the single malt market, such as it was, ignored it. As recently as 1989, the late Michael Jackson⁰ observed of Ardbeg that it 'has not operated since 1983, and its future must be in further doubt…' I recall visiting around then – the buildings were forlorn, desolate and cold, on the verge of dereliction, mouldering slowly in what Michael captured as a 'Gothic mood'.

How wrong can you be? So let's blast off! It's a journey to outer space.

* Thanks, Ardbeg. Keep 'em coming! ⁵Thanks *Whisky Advocate*. Keep 'em coming!
⁰ A highly respected, not to say revered and influential, writer on both beer and whisky.

Producer
Distillery
Visitor Centre
Availability

Grand Metropolitan
Midleton, Cork, Ireland
No
Like hen's teeth

BAILEYS'

THE
WHISKEY

DISTILLED IN IRELAND   alc 40%

Bailey's
The Whiskey

Can you imagine a Bailey's whiskey? No, neither can I. But, very briefly, there was one.

Back in 1997 some pretty smart people at Grand Metropolitan* thought it was just the thing to extend the Bailey's brand.

Grand plans were hatched for 'Bailey's The Whiskey' with the global launch scheduled for mid-1999, following test marketing in some Dublin pubs and off-licences. According to press reports, the product was to be sourced from Irish Distillers using the same blend as employed in the famous cream liqueur.

It was said to have involved 'two years of intensive research by a core team of up to 30 executives, researchers and designers and a spend to date of at least £500,000.' Bear in mind this was 1998. That's a tidy chunk of change. At £15.69 a bottle, this was to have been a premium whiskey and the firm belief was that it could command a significant market share.

Though based on the cream liqueur, the whiskey was said to represent 'a step forward within that tradition by extending the maturation process by up to six months in oak casks that once housed the Bailey's spirit blend. The result displays both the unmistakable character of great Irish whiskey and a distinctive nose, reminiscent of Bailey's Original Irish Cream.' In other words, it was to be 'finished' in casks that had previously held Bailey's Cream Liqueur – can you see where this is going?

Test marketing began in Dublin in March 1998. A top Bailey's executive told the *Irish Independent* newspaper: 'The only limitation on its potential would be if the tail started wagging the dog; in other words, if its success began to impact on the mother brand.'

But by June he had resigned, going on to found a vodka company. A bigger dog – Diageo – had barked and the Bailey's whiskey project was canned. The problem was those casks, which seemed to stretch, if not break, the rules on how whisky should be made. Strictly speaking those rules cover Scotch not Irish whiskey, but no one in the newly formed group wanted a fight with the Scotch Whisky Association (SWA) and a tiresome dispute over EU regulations.

In all the turmoil that accompanied the birth pangs of Diageo, the project was quickly forgotten. This is truly a legendary whiskey that enjoyed a short but doubtless happy life before being consigned to the corporate dustbin.

* The drinks conglomerate controlling International Distillers & Vintners, R&A Bailey, J&B, Gilbey's Smirnoff etc. that merged with Guiness in December 1997 to form Diageo.

4

Producer
Distillery
Visitor Centre

Availability

William Grant & Sons Distillers Ltd
Balvenie, Dufftown, Morayshire
Yes – but booking in advance
is necessary
Very limited

www.thebalvenie.com

Balvenie
50 Years Old

There are two entries for The Balvenie in this book, more than 30 years apart. One thing links them: a legend in his own right, David Stewart (remember him?) who has been with the company since he joined in August 1962 as a humble Stocks Clerk. 'Appears to be the solid type,' noted his original interviewer, concluding laconically if hardly enthusiastically that David 'would do'.

In fact, in his own modest and self-effacing way, he's done very well. It's hard to imagine a working life of 50 years in a single industry, let alone 50 years working for a single company. While such a thing may have been relatively commonplace in the early 20th century, such loyalty has slowly been crowded out by a faster-paced world.

The great and the good* of Scotch gathered at Balvenie maltings to acknowledge David's 50 years of service. A celebration, not a farewell it was marked by the launch of this 50-year-old dram with which we were able to toast the life and work of this very modest gentleman, one of Scotch whisky's true heroes.

If his early work remained low profile, in recent years he has received some much-deserved acclaim and, despite his well-known aversion to the limelight, David has been widely recognised by industry peers. He was awarded the Grand Prix of Gastronomy by the British Academy of Gastronomes (2005), as well as being conferred lifetime achievement awards from both the International Wine & Spirit Competition (2005) and the highly influential whisky magazine *Malt* (now *Whisky*) *Advocate* (2007), and given the Icon of Whisky award from *Whisky Magazine* (2009). The recognition of his peers was highlighted at the dinner by the presentation of a decanter by Richard Paterson of Whyte & Mackay engraved on behalf of his fellow judges at the IWSC.

David received this praise with modesty, referring to his love of experimentation with various whiskies and acknowledged that he found creating new expressions 'very satisfying'.

Balvenie 50 is a grand old gentleman with much life left in it. Rather like its Malt Master.

There were only 88 bottles made. We must have drunk several at the party, and they were followed by many other whiskies. I remember very little after that.

5

Producer
Distillery
Visitor Centre

Availability

William Grant & Sons Distillers Ltd
Balvenie, Dufftown, Morayshire
Yes – but booking in advance
is necessary
Auctions

www.thebalvenie.com

Balvenie Classic

Launched sometime in 1982, the Balvenie Classic has a place in history for – as far as anyone knows – this was the first whisky to be 'finished', that is to say, given an additional period of maturation in a second cask of a different type in order to impart extra flavour.

Now it's perfectly possible that people had been doing this before then, but no one has yet come forward to say so and, at the time, William Grant & Sons didn't make anything of it. This was just something that their legendary Malt Master* David Stewart had done to improve the whisky.

In this case Stewart used sherry butts to impart extra depth and richness to the finished product and, unwittingly, started a trend that has become almost routine. Today everyone offers a 'finish' and from all sorts of different casks. It's quite commonplace to visit a warehouse and see port pipes, rum puncheons and all kinds of wine casks, some bearing world-famous names.

When this was created, finishing was straightforward, but it has grown in such complexity that now a product like Dalmore's King Alexander III uses whiskies matured in ex-bourbon casks, Matusalem oloroso sherry wood, Madeira barrels, Marsala casks, port pipes and Cabernet Sauvignon wine barriques. And, with one exception, the term 'finish' has passed into general use, though Bruichladdich prefer to style whiskies managed in this way as having been ACEd – it stands for Additional Cask Evolution.

Classic, which appeared in two versions, one unaged and one at 18 Years Old, was eventually withdrawn in 1993 in favour of DoubleWood. Balvenie have followed this with a wide range and finishing has become very much their hallmark, with products such as Balvenie Rose (finished in port pipes), Port Wood (take a guess), 25 Year Old Triple Cask (oloroso sherry butts, first-fill bourbon barrels and traditional whisky casks), DoubleWood, TripleWood and so on.

So Classic has proved to be a very significant innovation, even if that wasn't fully appreciated at the time. With that in mind, I'm surprised it doesn't fetch higher prices at auction, especially when compared to the prices of more recent Balvenie expressions. Still, all the more for us to drink! You'll find it richly textured with great depth and smoothness.

A real classic.

6

Producer	Morrison Bowmore Distillers
Distillery	Bowmore, Islay
Visitor Centre	Yes
Availability	Auctions and specialists

BLACK BOWMORE

DISTILLED
1964

FINEST
ISLAY SINGLE MALT
SCOTCH WHISKY

DISTILLED AND BOTTLED IN SCOTLAND

MORRISON'S BOWMORE DISTILLERY
ISLAND OF ISLAY
SCOTLAND

70cl   50%vol

www.bowmore.com

Black Bowmore

The Bowmore distillery on Islay features here five times (six if you count Largiemeanoch), which is a measure of its status among whisky aficionados. Based on the reputation that started with Black Bowmore (and the very-much-more-limited bottling from the renowned Samaroli company*), the distillery has gone on to create some remarkable offerings. This is where it all began.

However, when the first release of this now-legendary whisky was made available in 1993, no one really gave it that much attention. I know of at least one Morrison Bowmore employee who, offered staff prices, baulked at the £80 that was asked. Others, perhaps alert to the astonishing quality, paid up – and drank their bottle (slowly, one hopes).

But today you might expect to pay well over £5,000 for this same bottle. It wasn't very long before word got out that it was – at its initial release – an astonishing bargain. But back then, Morrison Bowmore were more interested in selling large quantities of cheap whisky for the supermarket and own-label business. It was a very different business to the company we see today with their £100,000 bottles and hand-blown decanters.

In 1964, when this whisky was filled to cask, the Morrison family had only just acquired the distillery. At the time, the whisky industry used a much higher proportion of sherry casks than they do today. Black Bowmore is proof of the quality of some of that wood and the storage conditions in the famous No. 1 Warehouse, on the very edge of Bowmore's harbour. The whisky is extraordinarily concentrated, dense and intense in flavour, with a near-perfect balance of fruit, peat and power. Before long, Black Bowmore had justifiably acquired the 'legendary' tag and its reputation has grown with time.

Further releases followed in 1994 and 1995, all of which were greeted with considerable acclaim – and fetch similar prices. These are truly stellar whiskies.

In all probability, however, few will match this first release of the Black Bowmore for its combination of (initial) affordability, concentrated power and great finesse. If Bowmore never produced another legendary whisky (and it surely will) this would be an astonishing legacy and proof that the finest Scotch whisky offers a near-transcendental experience to those few lucky drinkers privileged to try it.

Do attempt at least one glass of this some time in your life, for it is a true legend.

* Keep going. You will learn more about them later.

7

Producer
Distillery
Visitor Centre
Availability

Morrison Bowmore Distillers
Bowmore, Islay
Yes
Distillery only

www.bowmore.com

Bowmore

1957

Back in 2003, writing about Bowmore for *Whisky Magazine*, I offered the following prophetic thought: 'Just 40 years ago you could buy an entire distillery for £117,000. On current trends, it won't be long before someone pays that for a single bottle of obscure malt.'

Truth to tell, I wasn't trying to be prophetic: I thought it was a rather droll idea. Stanley P. Morrison bought Bowmore for £117,000 in 1963 (and the price included a bond in Glasgow) – how outrageous that a single bottle could sell for this sort of money. However, I should have listened to myself and bought more old whisky because, with the Bowmore 1957, the prophecy has all but come true. Except, I add hastily, it's hardly 'obscure'.

This is the oldest Islay whisky ever bottled and the company made just 12 bottles, with the idea of keeping two, auctioning two in Edinburgh and New York in October 2012, and selling the remaining eight at the distillery, with all the net proceeds going to Scottish charities. As has become the norm, each was rather beautifully packaged in a hand-blown bottle with a platinum neck collar and stopper; hand-blown glasses and water jug; and a handmade presentation box of Scottish oak. And very handsome it looked.

Much PR hype followed but the auctions – rather embarrassingly – didn't go to plan. Both failed to reach the reserve of £100,000. Cue much *Schadenfreude* among rival distillers who had watched enviously (and slightly incredulously), and an outbreak of 'jumping the shark moment' comments on social media. I might have joined in.

But just before Christmas 2012 the distillery announced that the first bottle had been sold, with the buyer meeting the full asking price. Subsequently, I understand there have been further sales and Morrison Bowmore are confident that they will sell all ten bottles.

For good or bad, rare old whisky from renowned distilleries has entered a new and unexpected world, the domain of oligarchs and sheikhs (though they aren't supposed to drink, more than one of them is partial to a drop of the hard stuff). It's up there with customised Bugatti Veyrons, Patek Philippe Supercomplications and Candy & Candy London apartments.

I don't know whether to laugh or cry at a PR release which reads: 'This 54-year-old Bowmore 1957 is a symphony of aromas and flavours never before experienced.'

Well, I certainly haven't*.

8

Producer Morrison Bowmore Distillers
Distillery Bowmore, Islay
Visitor Centre Yes
Availability Auctions

www.bowmore.com

Bowmore

Bi-centenary

Remarkably, this whisky pre-dates the Black Bowmore that I mentioned just a few pages ago and that leads me to ask: why does one whisky command stellar prices while another (from the same distillery and generally agreed to be at least as good) fails to reach such heady heights?

Well, if I knew the answer to that I'd be very rich! But it does seem odd that you can still find (if you're lucky) this rather beautiful Bowmore, specially bottled for the distillery's bicentenary in 1979, for little more than £500 at auction, while the Black Bowmore releases have all pushed well through the four-figure barrier. In fact, you can easily pay ten times the price of this expression for Black Bowmore but – sticking my neck out – I suggest Black Bowmore is hardly ten times as good.

Though it doesn't carry an age statement, it isn't hard to imagine that the Morrison family (who owned the distillery at the time) sought out some very special casks for this bottling, as it was such a special occasion. Few distilleries in Scotland can claim to have been founded as early as Bowmore and the occasion was lavishly celebrated.

But there is no real mystery as to what the bottle contains, as a leaflet accompanies it stating: '*This bottle contains a vatting of the oldest stocks in the Bowmore Distillery. Some of it was distilled in 1950, twenty-nine years ago. In fact, the vatting contains whisky from ten different years between 1950 and 1966 – all very rare.*'

When Stanley P. Morrison bought Bowmore it was at something of a low ebb. He rapidly brought it back into production and, using sherry casks of exceptional quality, some legendary whisky was produced – noted for its depth of fruit, complexity of flavour and ability to age gracefully without becoming astringent or woody.

There's only one slightly alarming note: some commentators have suggested that the closures weren't of the highest quality, leading to excessive evaporation. In which case, I'd suggest you get right on and drink it rather than watching your whisky slowly disappear.

Tasting this for his wonderful WhiskyFun website, Serge Valentin from Malt Maniacs (a group of single malt enthusiasts who seem to have tasted every whisky under the sun) awarded it 96 points, remarking breathlessly: 'it's always an enchantment. What's really striking is the complexity of it all, every time you think you've found a particular aroma and try to put a name on it, it's another aroma that shows up and replaces it.'

That's worth £500 all on its own.

Luxurious

9

Producer
Distillery
Visitor Centre
Availability

Morrison Bowmore Distillers
Bowmore, Islay
Yes
Sold!

Bowmore
One of One

Here I am holding a £61,000 bottle of whisky. Fortunately, I grabbed it a few minutes before it was sold, otherwise I might not be looking so relaxed.

And it was largely luck that I picked up this particular bottle. Someone wanted to take my photograph* and, as a whisky auction was about to take place, it seemed like a good idea to include a bottle in the picture. As luck would have it, I was standing next to the 1964 48 Year Old Bowmore that had been created especially for the event – truly One of One and a legendary whisky.

Legendary because this turns out to be (at the time of writing) the most expensive bottle of Bowmore ever sold at auction; the highest price paid at auction in 2013; and the second-highest auction price ever for a bottle of whisky. Just as well I didn't drop it.

It was sold at a charity auction organised by The Worshipful Company of Distillers (that's their gong just visible round my neck) in London in October 2013. More than £250,000 was raised in just over an hour from a total of 55 lots, all donated by the whisky industry. This was the star lot.

The Worshipful Company of Distillers was founded in 1638 as one of the London Livery Companies. Today it exists mainly to raise charitable funds for various worthy causes. The auction was organised by the Company's Master, Brian Morrison, a former Chairman of Morrison Bowmore, and his old company stepped up with something quite special for the evening – as, in fairness, did a number of other companies and individuals.

I'm not normally a fan of these really expensive bottles but I do make an exception when the sale is for charity (like the Macallan Lalique Cire Perdue and M decanters and the 1957 Bowmore bottles). The bidding for all of the lots was fast and furious, with perhaps just an element of showmanship in some of the bids.

There is perhaps little to be learned from this, other than the pleasant conclusion that the licensed trade in general, and the whisky industry and its followers in particular, can be notably generous when the occasion arises. And that is something we can all celebrate.

I'd like to say that my hand was in the air during the bidding, but that would be a lie. But, as you can see, I did get both hands on the bottle.

10

Producer
Distillery
Visitor Centre
Availability

Diageo
Brora, Sutherland
Yes
Very limited

RARE MALT

NATURAL
CASK STRENGTH
SINGLE MALT
SCOTCH WHISKY

AGED **22** YEARS

DISTILLED IN 1972 AT THE

BRORA
DISTILLERY
ESTABLISHED 1819
BRORA SUTHERLAND

61.1%vol 70cle
PRODUCE OF SCOTLAND
LIMITED BOTTLING

Brora 1972
Rare Malts Edition

'There are no recorded instances of someone tasting this whisky and not being blown away,' says Edinburgh retailer Royal Mile Whiskies.

'One of the now-legendary 1972 Broras bottled by Diageo as part of the Rare Malts series, that really kick-started the explosion of interest in this lost distillery. 1972 is regarded by experts as a miracle year for Brora,' says the London-based specialist The Whisky Exchange. Malt Maniac Serge Valentin gave it 97 points (he doesn't do that often) and appeared so overcome that he couldn't write any notes (and that doesn't happen very often either, I can tell you).

But this whisky is not, in point of fact, from the distillery that we call Brora today, rather it is from its abandoned neighbour – the lost, forlorn and deeply lamented Clynelish (the nomenclature of these two gets confusing, so check it out online as I don't have room). And, if this 'kick-started the explosion of interest' then people hadn't been paying attention because Clynelish had been commended more than 90 years ago by Professor George Saintsbury and Aeneas MacDonald*. People in the know have always known that fine whisky was made here.

Despite that, it was closed in the late 1960s. It briefly reopened to produce a heavily peated spirit which was needed for the blending of Johnnie Walker, due to shortages of production on Islay. This Rare Malts expression dates from that period and is adored by enthusiasts of smoky whiskies.

It's curious to think that this whisky might never have existed were it not for a spell of very dry weather on Islay. Perhaps the whisky gods wanted this to be made as Clynelish's swansong. Production carried on after 1973 for another decade but peating levels were reduced and nothing quite as spectacular emerged ever again.

From time to time the cry is heard that the distillery should reopen. I can't see that happening. The future lies with very large, very efficient plants such as Roseisle. They may make a consistent product but somehow they lack the romance of a whisky such as this. Of such things are legends made.

Interestingly, when I asked a very senior, experienced and knowledgeable Diageo executive for his legendary whiskies this was the first one he picked. Without any hesitation whatsoever he recalled it instantly and was insistent that it should be included in this book. I'm happy to oblige.

* Don't pretend you don't know who they were – read on to find out.

11

Producer
Distillery
Visitor Centre
Availability

Bruichladdich Distillery Company
Bruichladdich, Islay
Yes
Specialists

www.bruichladdich.com

Bruichladdich

X4 Islay Spirit

Once upon a time – shortly before whisky became so tiresomely fashionable – a fellow by the name of Martin Martin* visited the Hebrides for his travel book *A Description of the Western Islands of Scotland* (in 1695 – OK, so it was quite a long time before whisky became fashionable). While there, he claims to have encountered a quadruple-distilled whisky known as 'usquebaugh-baul' – the ultimate whisky.

'The first taste affects all the members of the body,' he wrote excitedly. 'Two spoonfuls of this last liquor is a sufficient dose; and if any man should exceed this, it would presently stop his breath and endanger his life.' If you think about it, that's one hell of a tasting note. In fact, his words are legendary in their own right as they almost certainly make up the first tasting note ever. They've gone downhill ever since, if you ask me (but read on for a classic).

Three hundred years later, Bruichladdich, being Bruichladdich, decided to recreate usquebaugh-baul (which they translated as 'Perilous Whisky') as a 92% abv spirit. They had to distil it four times to get to that mighty level of alcohol, so they called it X4. Predictably enough, the SWA (best friends of Bruichladdich's PR Department) condemned it as 'irresponsible', thus ensuring further coverage.

What they thought of Bruichladdich's next stunt isn't recorded but, in August 2008, for the BBC TV programme *Oz and James Drink to Britain* three litres of this fearsome liquid was used to fuel a Radical SR4 racing car, which James May proceeded to drive at 90mph plus around Islay's Lochindaal coast road (people and sheep were cleared first).

What a hoot! As ever with Bruichladdich, though, there was a point. They were experimenting, having fun with whisky and challenging some conventions at the same time. And strange things happen: one doesn't think of James May as a poetic type of chap and yet, on trying X4 in the distillery warehouse and confessing that whisky takes him to a dark place, he responded that this provided 'a moment of great clarity… you see the clouds parting and rain lifting.' This, concluded May and fellow presenter Oz Clarke, was the Spirit of Hope found at the bottom of Pandora's Box, if you only dare open it.

Today some specialists still carry the original X4 Islay Spirit (it's not whisky as it wasn't aged for the mandatory three years) and a slightly tamed version, X4+3, which has been and is therefore legally whisky. Try it if you dare – but don't say you haven't been warned!

Speaking of tasting notes, try this: 'Not cooking oil. Not diesel oil. Sewing machine oil.' © 2010 Charles McLean in *The Times*.

* Martin Martin – so good they named him twice.

12

Producer
Distillery
Visitor Centre
Availability

Living

Wm Cadenhead Ltd
n/a
Shops across Europe
As above and online

www.wmcadenhead.com

Cadenhead's

It's not really possible to write about whisky legends without some mention of the merchant and bottler William Cadenhead. Established in 1842 they are Scotland's oldest firm of this type, today controlled by J & A Mitchell & Co. Ltd, the same private owners behind the Springbank Distillery. They acquired the business when it ran into difficulties in 1972. All the stock had been sold at auction – then the largest sale of wines and spirits ever held in Great Britain – and, though Mitchell bought the name, goodwill and original shop, there was much to do to rebuild the firm.

But it was in good hands and by concentrating on single malt whiskies and fine rum, and never chill-filtering or colouring their releases, a reputation was built up among connoisseurs and enthusiasts who appreciated this approach, unfashionable though it was at the time. The shops still present a somewhat old-fashioned appearance but do not be fooled – the people behind the counter know and love their products and approach their job with real enthusiasm.

Several of their private bottlings have achieved very high marks in independent tastings and would now be keenly sought after if they were ever to appear in auction (they won't; anyone owning one of these will be keeping it). One might mention the 18-year-old Longrow 1974 bottling released for Cadenhead's 150th Anniversary, or the Laphroaig 15 Year Old from a sherry cask (1967 distillation – one of this Islay distillery's finest expressions) in its squat dark brown bottle. Do not let looks deceive you; modest and unassuming they may be, particularly in contrast to today's elaborate presentations, these are stellar whiskies, upon which an unrivalled reputation has been built.

In style and approach, then, Cadenhead's stand almost alone. Interestingly, family firms generally seem to adopt this lower profile, less driven by fashion and the passing trends: one thinks of Glenfarclas, Gordon & Macphail and Cadenhead's parent J & A Mitchell & Co. Ltd with their Springbank and Longrow.

Today the firm offers a number of 'Collections', including some obscure world whiskies in their range. Who knows: perhaps something from Tasmania will be a legend of the future?

'By Test the Best' wrote an early proprietor and this remains the firm's motto to this day.

13

Producer
Distillery
Visitor Centre
Availability

Luxurious

Chivas Brothers Ltd
n/a – this is a blend
At Strathisla
In your dreams

Chivas Regal
25 Years Old (Original bottling)

You can buy a Chivas Regal 25 Years Old blend today, and very lovely it is, too. But what you may not know is that the original Chivas Brothers of Aberdeen first introduced their Chivas Regal brand to the USA in 1909 as a 25 Years Old, where it was an immediate success. This, then, has an excellent claim to be the world's first luxury whisky. Depending on how you look at it, it has a lot to answer for.

Unfortunately, a combination of Prohibition (the US was its main market), the world's Great Depression and the advancing age of the partners in Chivas Brothers meant that the last of this pioneering blend was bottled in the late 1920s. That, so far as anybody knew, was that. The general view in the whisky trade was that whisky as old as 25 years was past its best. With very few exceptions (for example, King's Ransom, which I discuss later) luxury blends were a thing of the past.

Chivas Brothers was sold in 1936 to a partnership led by Stanley P. Morrison (later of Morrison Bowmore fame) and the remaining stocks were sold off. In 1949, what remained of the company was purchased by Samuel Bronfman of The Seagram Company Ltd and two years later they purchased Strathisla Distillery and went about rebuilding the Chivas Regal legend.

That, of course, they did with the 12 Years Old expression but it was not until 2007 (with the brand now under the ownership of Pernod Ricard – confusing, isn't it?) that the 25 Years Old expression returned to the market.

Naturally, a few bottles of the original version have survived. They're very rare, part of whisky's history and a bona fide collector's item. If I had one I don't think I could bear to open and drink it: it would be like scratching my name on to one of the standing stones at Stonehenge. In a small and entirely trivial way, drinking one of these venerable bottles would be a crime against all humanity. So it follows that there's little point in actually owning it: like the blue whale, it's enough to know that it's there*.

For what it's worth, I can assure you that the current version is very, very good.

* If you do happen to own one, please look after it. The whisky, obviously. It would be silly to try to keep a whale, whatever its colour.

45

14

Producer Chivas Brothers Ltd
Distillery n/a – this is a blend
Visitor Centre At Strathisla
Availability Auctions

www.chivas.com

Chivas Regal
Royal Salute 50 Years Old

Why this and not the Royal Salute Tribute to Honour? It's entirely a personal view but, comparing the two, I find this a more elegant and restrained presentation. I thought the Tribute to Honour was rather vulgar and over the top (sorry, Chivas) but, then again, a leading retailer that I spoke to considered it lacked shelf appeal and wasn't nearly 'bling' enough. I would like to imagine the choice comes down to my exquisitely refined taste but I have to admit he knows a great deal more than me about what the market for this type of thing requires. Still, it's my book.

This, then, was produced in 2003 to commemorate Queen Elizabeth II's 50th as monarch and, naturally, the 50th anniversary of the launch of Royal Salute. It's been a remarkably successful brand for Chivas Brothers who have expanded the range over the years. From the original and well-loved 21 Years Old style, they now offer the delights of The Hundred Cask Selection, 38 Years Old Stone of Destiny, and the 62 Gun Salute expressions*.

Of course, this 50-year-old style has been rather overtaken by the rash of special releases to commemorate Her Majesty's recent 60th anniversary, as the Scotch whisky industry went into overdrive to mark the occasion with their finest whiskies. But there were only ever 255 bottles produced of the 50 Years Old expression; the first being presented to Sir Edmund Hillary to mark the coincidental anniversary of his pioneering ascent of Mount Everest§.

Ironically, Chivas appear to have used up all their very old whiskies as they were unable to offer anything more sensational, expensive and exclusive for the 60th anniversary than the regular 21 Years Old blend in a limited edition bottle and box. That seems rather an unfortunate irony for a firm whose key message about whisky is 'Age Matters'.

The distillers themselves summarised this 50 Years Old whisky as representing 'unrivalled excellence'. I should hope so: my first house cost less.

* I once stood through a full 62-gun salute at the Tower of London. It was very noisy and they all sounded the same.
§ In case you're worried that some discrimination went on here, I can reassure you that Hilary's climbing partner Tenzing Norgay had died in 1986. I checked.

15

Producer
Distillery
Visitor Centre
Availability

Diageo
Convalmore, Dufftown, Morayshire
No
Limited

Convalmore
28 Years Old

I've decided to declare this a legend, despite the fact that this will now push the price completely out of my reach; for this is one of the most extraordinary whiskies you'll ever drink (or not, now).

Three thousand, nine hundred bottles were released in 2005 by Diageo as part of their Special Releases series. It wasn't a great success, probably because no one knew or cared very much about Convalmore; it isn't fashionable and there aren't very many merchant expressions to compare. For a while you could pick up bottles for £100–£150: still a lot of money for a bottle of whisky but, in truth, something of a bargain. Today, on whisky specialists' sites where it's still available, it's pushing £500, and the latest Special Release (only the second they've done from this distillery) is nearly £600.

Convalmore is in Dufftown. It opened in 1893 but was absorbed by the original Distillers Company Limited as part of the industry rationalisation of the 1920s and 1930s. Today it forms part of the William Grant & Sons' site, also home to Glenfiddich, The Balvenie and Kininvie. You can see Convalmore, looking abandoned and somewhat forlorn, as you drive by, but I doubt anyone really gives it a second glance.

Why would you? It hasn't distilled since it was closed in 1985 and it will never distil again. Most of the plant has been removed and the buildings sold to William Grant & Sons, though Diageo retain the distillery licence. Virtually all of the whisky produced here was used in blending: no one except Diageo knows how much is left and they're not saying. One thing's for sure – prices for this will rise as stocks run out and word spreads of its remarkable quality.

But it's not simply about rarity. As this exceptional and grossly underrated dram reveals, occasionally some very special whisky was produced here. This is utterly delicious: even at cask strength (a mighty 57.9%) there is a creamy mouth feel and a beguiling waxiness to the whisky that defies explanation.

It's a sensation more than a flavour. You may also encounter it in some Clynelish (look for the Brora Rare Malts entry) and in very good Irish pot still whiskies, but it is highly unusual and beloved of the connoisseur. The waxiness may come from a build-up of residue in the wash and spirit chargers, or possibly from an accumulation of material in the neck of the stills – no one is quite sure but it has been noticed that, if this is removed, the spirit character changes and some waxiness is lost.

Put like that it doesn't sound very nice. Trust me, though, it is. Shame the price is going to rocket.

Producer
Distillery
Visitor Centre
Availability

The Edrington Group
n/a – this is a blend
n/a
Widespread

Cutty Sark

We should, of course, be careful about chucking terms like 'legendary' and 'iconic' around too easily, lest they lose all meaning. This is not a press release after all.

You can buy a bottle of Cutty Sark fairly easily for around £20. It's not that difficult to find and there's no danger that they will run out. So I thought long and hard before including it here. Why, you might reasonably ask, should this be considered 'legendary'?

Well, few brands ever take whisky off in new directions. Most represent a cautious, evolutionary approach. That's inevitable for a product that takes a minimum of three years to come to maturity, with heavy capital investment required to produce let alone launch it. And, for the most part, whisky drinkers are creatures of habit*.

Back in 1923, the wine merchants Berry Bros & Rudd broke away from the prevailing orthodoxy to launch a whisky that was easy-drinking, light in both flavour and colour, and ideal for cocktails or mixed drinks. Eschewing the advice of focus groups (or whatever passed for a focus group in 1923) they put it in a cheery green glass bottle with a bright yellow label. And, doubtless to confound traditionalists, they called it Scots Whisky.

It was an instant success, taking the number one sales position in the USA once Prohibition was repealed. In an age when every case was packed by hand, it sold over 1 million cases. But, by the 1980s it had faded as competitors like Johnnie Walker, Dewar's and Chivas Regal gained ground. For a long time it seemed as if Cutty Sark would be relegated to the footnotes of history.

Today, the drab, conformist hand of legislation demands that it be referred to as Scotch, but the cheery packaging is still there, albeit slightly modernised. A change in ownership and a sustained effort to revive the brand have meant that today it is fighting back. It is marketed as an irreverent alternative to traditional Scotch. Whisky's slightly stuffy image as something preferred by older men may itself be something of a myth but Cutty is sharp, urban and *happening*.

Indeed, Cutty's new Prohibition expression takes the brand off in another different direction, in a nod to its legendary role in the days of America's 'great experiment'.

I daresay Al Capone would have approved.

* I realise, of course, that you are young at heart, adventurous and always ready for new experiences. I was talking about all the other boring, fuddy-duddy whisky drinkers.

17

Producer
Distillery

Visitor Centre
Availability

Reid & Colville & Co
Dalintober, Cambeltown, Argyll
and Bute
No
Auctions, but highly unlikely

Dalintober

Dalintober is one of the lost distilleries of Campbeltown. Most of the site is gone, with houses on the land: though some old walls remain, their stones are silent.

Aeneas MacDonald, the most poetic of whisky writers (of whom much more later), thought the Campbeltown whiskies were 'the double basses of the whisky orchestra' – a typically lyrical description, which he was, I think, the first to employ. He lamented the decline of the Campbeltown industry, even though ten distilleries remained in operation at the date of his book. What riches we have lost!

By the time he was writing (1930), Dalintober had closed forever. It had been established by Messrs Reid and Colville in 1823 and, according to the noted Victorian commentator Alfred Barnard, 'Dalintober signifies the valley of the wells.' The distillery was working when he visited it, producing some 120,000 gallons (around 545,000 litres) of Campbeltown malt annually. He evidently considered it important, allocating two full pages and a full page illustration to his account of his visit.

In 1919 it changed hands, being purchased by the West Highland Malt Distilleries Ltd who, following the general slump in trade in the 1920s, closed it in 1925. Dalintober was never to work again.

Strangely, though, some of its output was bottled as single malt and at an unusually great age. At the time this was pretty much unheard of. A whisky from the 1868 distillation, bottled in 1908, was auctioned by Christie's in November 1990 for £2,530. Why a 40-year-old cask survived and was bottled at that age remains a mystery.

Even more interestingly, a few years ago there was a bottle of Dalintober in the old visitor centre at the Tamdhu Distillery on Speyside*. Charles Craig mentions this in his invaluable *Scotch Whisky Industry Record* (1994) so we may be sure that my memory and other accounts of this furtive bottle are not in error. But some years later it had 'disappeared'. Perish the thought that it was purloined by some light-fingered scoundrel. If so, it is the whisky equivalent of a stolen masterpiece by Rembrandt, forever destined to hang unseen in a hall of shame. Perhaps conscience may eventually prevail and the bottle will be surreptitiously returned – but, in the meantime, Tamdhu has changed hands, so the new owners may dispute with Edrington (who operated Tamdhu previously) who is the rightful custodian. One thing is certain: it would be worth a great deal more than £2,530.

It was described by MacDonald as 'potent, full-bodied, and pungent' – but I don't suppose any of us will ever really know.

18

Producer
Distillery
Visitor Centre
Availability

Lost

Wright & Greig
Dallas Dhu, Forres, Morayshire
Yes, today it is a museum
Occasional specialists

www.historic-scotland.gov.uk

Dallas Dhu

Dallas Dhu, or Dallasmore as it was to be known, was a creation of the great whisky boom of the late 19th century. Built in 1898, it was immediately sold on to the Glasgow blenders Wright & Greig who renamed it in honour of their Roderick Dhu brand, then a popular blended whisky.

Roderick Dhu is a central character in Sir Walter Scott's lengthy narrative poem *The Lady of the Lake*. Enormously influential at the time (both Rossini and Schubert were inspired by it), the name would have been a potent one to 19th century audiences*.

Unfortunately, the distillery opened just as the great whisky boom turned to bust. Subsequently, it had something of a difficult life under different owners, ending up as part of the Distillers Company Ltd. They finally closed it in March 1983 during a wave of rationalisations. In 1998 it was reopened to the public as a museum and today it is operated by Historic Scotland.

They maintain everything in splendid order and it's easy to imagine as you stroll round that the distillery could reopen at very short notice. That's unlikely, in fact, because, apart from the fact that it doesn't have a distilling licence anymore, much of the equipment would be unlikely to meet health and safety standards. However, it's a wonderful time capsule and great fun to visit.

As distilling continued until 1983 and a considerable amount of stock appears to have found its way to third party bottlers, it is possible – at a price – to enjoy the whisky still. Not the original Roderick Dhu blend, of course, as stocks ran out years ago, though some of the splendid pottery jugs and other promotional items for the brand seem to turn up fairly frequently on eBay.

No, what you can try is Dallas Dhu's single malt. It's been bottled by Diageo as part of the old Rare Malts series and by third party bottlers and merchants, such as Master of Malt, Douglas Laing, Gordon & Macphail, Historic Scotland, Signatory, Cadenhead's and the Scotch Malt Whisky Society. Prices range upwards from around £200. Given the current cult following for silent and closed distilleries, prices seem likely to go up.

But if £200 seems a little steep, then last time I was there the gift shop was offering the Roderick Dhu blend (as recreated for Historic Scotland) for around £20. It's a perfectly pleasant and inoffensive way to end your tour and better than a cup of tea.

* I haven't read it, of course.

19

Producer
Distillery
Visitor Centre
Availability

Whyte & Mackay Ltd
Dalmore, Alness, Ross-shire
Yes
Specialists and possibly at auction

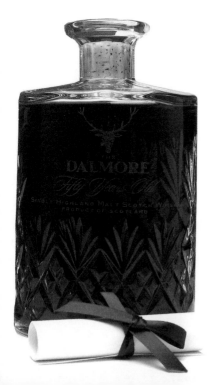

www.thedalmore.com

Dalmore

50 Years Old

One can't deny Dalmore's diligent pursuit of the ultra-premium market. As well as the Trinitas (which naturally gets its very own entry) they have a veritable galaxy of expressions at ever higher prices – Eos, Selene, Constellation, Aurora, Astrum and so on and so forth. And that's not to mention the Richard Paterson Collection, available at the time of writing from Harrods for as near to £1 million as makes no difference (12 bottles, though, and a pretty cabinet in which to keep them).

But before their prices really rocketed, they did release some older whiskies, including several batches of a 50 Years Old expression. You can find it in a black, ceramic, decanter-style bottle, which was produced around 1976, and the version illustrated here, which came to the market a couple of years later at twice the price (nicer package, though).

Since then the distillery has been through a bewildering series of changes of owners. As I write, it appears to be about to be swallowed up into the Diageo empire*, who, of course, already have their own views on the ultra-premium market, addressing this mainly through very limited Johnnie Walker expressions. At one level down they have Mortlach, so the future for Dalmore, especially at this elevation, seems unclear.

It's only one man's opinion, of course, but my own sense is that Whyte & Mackay always tried a little too hard for comfort; protesting just a little too stridently and with such extravagant language that I began to doubt the whole basis of their claims. There's no doubt this is very fine whisky (if you like them old, dark and rich) but when I read on their website that one whisky was 'a unique creation worthy of the ancient gods themselves', I was forced to conclude that the author got rather over-excited and needed to lie down for a while in a darkened room. That's just one example: I could quote more but they don't need any encouragement.

Being a simple soul, I also find some of their cask finishing a little hard to follow and the claim that the very oldest bottlings contain whisky dating back to June 1868 strains credulity. Perhaps I should think of it as coming from the equivalent of a homeopathic whisky vat.

In fairness, Serge Valentin of the Malt Maniacs praised this to the skies, awarding it 96 points. It ought to be good, though, at £15,000: you can buy a house in parts of England for that[§].

* Competition authorities permitting. § Not a very nice one admittedly; you'd hardly even keep students in it.

20

Producer
Distillery
Visitor Centre
Availability

Whyte & Mackay Ltd
Dalmore, Alness, Ross-shire
Yes
Improbable

www.thedalmore.com

Dalmore

Trinitas

Well, they got what they wanted, I suppose.

The Dalmore Trinitas was released to a blaze of publicity in October 2010 in an edition of three. Much was made of the exclusive, limited number of bottles, and the fact that Dalmore had pre-sold one (or two – accounts seem to vary) prior to the release. The third bottle ended up in Harrods, who sold it for £125,000.

A storm of controversy followed which was, of course, the general idea. Dalmore was being 'repositioned' as a luxury brand, following in the footsteps of The Macallan, where Dalmore's David Robertson had previously worked. The Apprentice seemed determined to become the Master. Aided by Whyte & Mackay's ebullient Master Blender Richard Paterson and supported by Whyte & Mackay's then-owner, the flamboyant Dr Vijay Mallya, nothing was to stand in the way of their ambition to deliver the most expensive whisky in the world.

Perhaps that sounds rather vulgar. It must be acknowledged that there is hard-nosed commercial logic behind it. The marketing theory of 'trickle-down' or 'image cascade' holds that the status of the highest-priced products in a range will reflect on lesser offerings, making them more desirable and allowing the brand owner to massage all prices upwards. As if on cue, a mob of gullible hacks, bloggers and assorted journalists all breathlessly repeated the hype, performing a synchronised ballet of ecstatic hyperbole like drugged, robotic puppets or some helpless rabbit mesmerised by a weasel's hypnotic dance.

Those commentators criticising this inflationary trend were equally pawns in Dalmore's wily game. Negative coverage merely heightened and served the controversy.

Certain questions were never answered. For example, the blend is said to contain whisky from 1868, 1878 and 1926. I'm sure it does. But simply quoting a year of distillation tells us little until it is revealed when that whisky was placed in glass. Because at that point it stops aging and, as long as you wait, it is still only that age. And, of course, there is no information on how much of this venerable spirit went into the final blend.

I have to stop now, because I'm doing their work for them. There's no denying that this was a success, however much it pains me to admit it.

In the course of researching this book I met one of the three people who own a bottle of Trintitas and he seemed utterly delighted with his purchase. Didn't offer me any, though.

Not even a sniff of the cork.

21

Producer
Distillery
Visitor Centre
Availability

John Dewar & Sons Ltd
n/a – this is a blend
Aberfeldy Distillery
Widespread

www.dewars.com

Dewar's
White Label

Surely there's been a mistake here? This is a bottle of a mainstream, standard blend, widely available, especially in the USA where it has long been a favourite.

How, you ask (not unreasonably), can this be described as a legend?

In essence this represents the great blended whiskies which make up more than 90% of all the Scotch whisky that is sold around the world. Without these we would never be able to enjoy the incredible variety of different whiskies that confront us every time we drop into our favourite whisky specialist or browse whisky porn on the web. You can be pretty certain that your favourite single malt, especially if it's an obscure one, would have long been consigned to history were it not for the amazing platform provided by blends such as this.

You may think blends are ubiquitous, unadventurous and possibly even bland and boring*, but they are the key to understanding the richness and diversity of the whisky market. So salute them!

This also allows me to mention Sir Thomas 'Tommy' Dewar, one of the original 'whisky barons', the flamboyant, buccaneering entrepreneurial genii who at the end of the 19th century built their respective family firms into the largest and most successful in the industry. In the process, Tommy and his brother John became very wealthy, established and politically successful, before merging their firm into the Distillers Company in 1925. Today it is owned by Bacardi.

In 1894, Tommy set off on a two-year, round-the-world sales trip, appointing new agents and opening new markets. Ever the self-publicist, he wrote a successful account of his travels on his return. The White Label blend was developed by Dewar's, with the assistance of their first Master Blender A. J. Cameron, an early pioneer of marrying whiskies to ensure consistent flavour.

The blend has won many awards and has long been noted for its consistency. In fact, for many years it was marketed with the slogan 'never varies'.

More recently, premium Dewar's blends have been added to the portfolio and excellent they are, too. All are typified by the softer, sweeter palate of Aberfeldy single malt (from the first distillery built by the Dewar brothers), a contrasting style to the more robust West Coast smokiness evident in competitors, such as Johnnie Walker.

Commonplace it may be, but this is a legendary whisky. I suggest that you try some for yourself and see why it has won so many awards. It's not expensive.

* And you'd be wrong.

22

Producer
Distillery
Visitor Centre
Availability

Drambuie Liqueur Company
n/a – this is a blend
No
Widespread

www.drambuie.com

Drambuie

15 Years Old Speyside Liqueur

When I started making my list of legendary whiskies, I began by thinking about what famous Scots would have drunk: people like Robert Burns, Robert Louis Stevenson, Alexander Graham Bell, John Logie Baird, Groundskeeper Willie and so on. That naturally led me to Bonnie Prince Charlie (that's him opposite). He reputedly passed on the recipe for his secret liqueur to the MacKinnon family on the Isle of Skye as a reward for sheltering him from the Duke of Cumberland's troops following the disastrous (for him) Battle of Culloden. No cash, you notice, just a recipe. Scotsmen!

Following Culloden there was a huge bounty on the Prince's head and he was an outlaw; a desperate man quite literally in fear of his life. We may imagine the effect of the cold West Highland rain harshly driving this band of royal fugitives onwards, sheltering where they could from relentless, unforgiving pursuers tracking them across bleak heather and bare moorland. An occasional draught of Charlie's rare elixir no doubt heartened the group. Perhaps it even banished – if only for a few short moments – uncomfortable memories and speculations, and comforted the loyal followers and spurred them on to effect the Prince's eventual, near-miraculous escape.

After keeping the recipe a secret for many, many years, the MacKinnon family, so the story goes, began marketing Drambuie in the early part of the 20th century – Drambuie being a corruption of the Gaelic 'an dram buideach' or 'the drink that satisfies'.

I know that liqueurs are rather out of fashion, disparagingly referred to as 'stickies' and served, if they are served at all, only at the end of a dinner party, but Drambuie has moved on – at least with their 15 Year Old Speyside version. It is very tasty – a sort of ready-made Rusty Nail in a bottle. I call it 'the whisky drinker's liqueur' and I wholeheartedly recommend that you try it.

Assuming that you know what a bottle of Drambuie looks like, I have decided to illustrate this entry with the rather charming wood engraving of Bonnie Prince Charlie by Chris Daunt that you see here. It graced the pages of a tiny book that I wrote for Drambuie to go in their Drambuie Jacobite expression – only 150 were made* because it was rather special, but I've always thought it a shame that this lovely picture hasn't enjoyed wider recognition.

Bonnie Prince Charlie is a legendary figure from Scottish history and his Drambuie enjoys similar status. I could even start to tell you what's in it, but then I would have to kill you.

* They were £3,500 a bottle – so no surprise that they're rather precious. Though, if I say so myself, they did include a *very nice* book.

23

Producer
Distillery
Visitor Centre
Availability

Lost

Duncan Forbes of Culloden
Ryefield, Ferintosh, Black Isle
No
None

www.ferintosh.org

Ferintosh

Thee, Ferintosh! O sadly lost!
Scotland lament thee frae coast to coast!

Burns' lines on the Ferintosh concession are well known. Taken from his poem 'Scotch Drink' (1785), Burns was lamenting the decision by the United Kingdom Parliament to cancel the privileges granted in 1689 by the old Scots Parliament to Duncan Forbes of Culloden whose Ryefield distillery had been destroyed by Jacobite soldiers under Graham of Claverhouse, Viscount Dundee. The Forbes were, of course, staunch Presbyterians, opposed to the Catholic Jacobites.

In compensation, Forbes was permitted to distil free of duty the grain grown on his own Ferintosh estate. Thus empowered he was able to sell a superior quality product cheaper than his competitors and with the profits he enlarged said estates. By the 1770s his descendants were making substantial profits and operating four distilleries. Naturally their competitors cried foul and in 1784, as part of the Wash Act, the privilege was withdrawn. The Forbes family was compensated to the tune of £22,500 but, by now too grand to engage in 'trade', their distilleries were closed.

The name lives on, however, immortalised by Burns who is demonstrating in this poem the symbolic importance to Scotland of its national drink and thus Ferintosh is part of the rich cultural hinterland that makes the study of whisky so rewarding. Later, acknowledging this, other distillers were to adopt the Ferintosh name as a brand for their whisky (sadly, fully taxed), though without conspicuous success. Various ventures failed, including the original Ben Wyvis, which operated in Dingwall from 1879 to 1926, having been renamed Ferintosh in 1893.

Perhaps the name is now jinxed. That would be fitting. Born in flame and riot, immortalised in verse and mired in controversy, Ferintosh deserves its legendary, almost mythic, status. But, were it to rise again, it could surely never reach such levels of esteem. Considered as a lost giant, almost any claim can be made for Ferintosh. But let's leave the last word with Burns, who had this to say about his beloved whisky:

... oil'd by thee,
The wheels of life gae down-hill, scrievin,
Wi' rattlin glee.

24

Producer
Distillery
Visitor Centre

Availability

Lost

Friar John Cor
Lindores Abbey, Newburgh, Fife
No, just a heap of stones in a field
(private property)
None

Friar John Cor's

Aquavite

'Et per liberacionem factam Fratri Johanni Cor per preceptum compotorum rotulatoris, ut asserit, de mandato domini regis ad faciendum aquavite, infra hoc compotum viij bolle brasii.'

OK? Got that?

In every whisky book under the sun you can read about a mysterious 'eight bolls of malt'* and a fellow called Friar John Cor, reputedly Scotland's first distiller. Only here you also get a picture of the Exchequer Rolls of Scotland (1494–95, Vol. X, page 487, to be exact, covering 1st June 1494) which is where he and his bolls are first mentioned. Are you any the wiser?

Thought not. Despite reading about this it doesn't really mean anything. His fellow monks might have been drinking the good Friar's elixir, or it might have been needed for embalming fluid, or for disinfectant, perfume or even to help make gunpowder (King James IV was a bit of an amateur chemist apparently and rather keen on gunpowder). Fact is, this enigmatic entry in the royal household accounts (for that's basically what they were) confuses rather than enlightens. It's been calculated that eight bolls would make around 350 litres of pure alcohol today, but that's with sophisticated equipment, so let's halve that. Such a quantity suggests this wasn't the first attempt, so distilling in Scotland's monasteries can confidently be dated to some years earlier.

But then there's an Irish reference to distilling from 1405 and the process of distilling is mentioned in Chaucer's *Canterbury Tales* (around 1387–1394) where the Canon Yeoman refers to alembics and *descensories* (a sort of flask or retort).

However, as any academic knows, it's not the person who discovers something who gets the fame but the fellow who gets it written up in the best journals and Friar John Cor certainly leads the pack here.

When it suits the Scotch whisky industry to bring him out, they do so with relish (there was a rather nice 500th anniversary blend released by James Buchanan & Co. in 1994 and Robertson's of Pitlochry bottled some 10-year-old Strathmill as Friar John Cor) but when the owners of Lindores Abbey tried to pass round the hat to raise funds for restoration and even a visitor centre the industry was posted missing in action. There is a plan to open a distillery there now, though – let's hope it works out.

Sadly, Friar John Cor's memory is everyone's property and thus no one's. Still, he and his bolls of malt are a legend, even if a misunderstood one. But embalming fluid? Disinfectant? That's certainly a taste you wouldn't forget.

* It's a measure of weight – about 500kg.

67

25

Producer George Washington
Distillery Mount Vernon, Virginia, USA
Visitor Centre Yes
Availability Limited batch availability

www.mountvernon.org/distillery

George Washington's
Mount Vernon Whiskey

George Washington, the man who as President of the United States imposed a tax on whiskey and started a revolution which took 13,000 armed troops to suppress, was himself a distiller.

And not just some amateur, Friday night, 'I'll try anything' home distiller but, at the time, the largest and most profitable distiller in America. Of course, it took a Scotsman to show him how it was done.

That was James Anderson who in 1797 travelled from Spencerfield Farm in Fife* to be Washington's farm manager. Seeing Washington's go-ahead attitude and his interest in a profitable business, Anderson proposed taking the produce of the extensive estate and starting a distillery. By 1799 they were working five stills and making around 11,000 gallons a year. Unfortunately, shortly after Washington's death, the distillery closed down and was subsequently destroyed in a fire.

That would have been that, except archaeological work in 1999 managed to show the extent of the distillery and in 2007 a painstakingly accurate, full-size working replica was opened. Today you can visit the site, tour the distillery and buy a rye whiskey that approximates to Washington's original recipe of 60% rye, 35% corn and 5% malted barley. Be aware, it's not cheap: $95. And I'd say you're probably paying around $20 for the whiskey and $75 to fund the site. Which is fair enough, just don't expect it to taste like a $95 bottle.

There is a huge amount of information on the Mount Vernon website, with the usual intensely earnest desire prevalent among American museum folk to get every detail correct. It's a shame then that they didn't get someone from Scotland to listen to the actor playing James Anderson in the otherwise excellent video – his accent is located somewhere in the Irish Sea, veering off into a Dublin pub once in a while. Combined with his piratical leer it lends unintended comic effect to what was clearly a well-researched and thoroughly absorbing little film.

As for the whiskey, well, as a 'white whiskey' it's basically perfectly legal while being spiritually close to moonshine but, because of the Washington connection and his part in American whiskey history, part of a legend all the same.

* Strangely enough, a whisky company still works from Spencerfield, where Jane and Alex Nicol of Spencerfield Spirits, noted for their Sheep Dip whisky and Edinburgh Gin, hatch their cunning plots for world domination.

[6] I now expect a furious email from Mount Vernon's philologist reprimanding me and outlining in pedantic detail the proof that 18th-century Scots spoke like Irishmen! I'm sure they'll be right, it sounds funny, that's all.

26

Producer
Distillery
Visitor Centre
Availability

William Grant & Sons Distillers Ltd
Girvan, Ayrshire
No
Specialists

www.grantswhisky.com

Girvan
Single Grain

This is the story of a man and a distillery. Not, as you might expect, William Grant and the distillery he built (Glenfiddich), but Charles Grant Gordon, the fourth generation of that remarkable family, and the distillery he built: Girvan.

Girvan is just as important to the story of Scotch whisky as Glenfiddich, and Charles Grant Gordon every bit as much a legend as his forefather but, sadly, both are less well known. Yet it can be argued that he saved the firm and created the basis on which it flourishes today as an independent, family-owned business.

Back in the early 1960s the Scotch whisky industry was dominated by the Distillers Company Ltd, then managed in a very conservative (some would say old-fashioned) manner. They took a somewhat patrician view of their competitors and were used to the idea that what was good for the DCL was good for Scotch.

Right from its launch, they let it be known that they were opposed to the advertising of whisky brands on the new-fangled commercial television channel that had launched in London in 1955* and woe betide anyone who broke ranks.

But Grant's needed to promote their Stand Fast blend (today known as Family Reserve). In 1962, they decided TV was the future. Somehow the idea then got about that, by some strange quirk of fate, the DCL would be unable – with the greatest of regret, naturally – to supply any grain whisky to Grants the following year. Without those supplies there could be no blend and Grants would be unable to satisfy the thirsty customers whipped up by the commercials.

However, nothing daunted, Charles Gordon found a site near Girvan close to a deep-water port convenient for supplies of US maize beside the ruins of a WW2 munitions factory, and in 1963 he built his own grain distillery in nine months flat.

That was an astonishing achievement. Today, Girvan is a huge complex incorporating grain, single malt and gin distilling, and a massive warehouse development. By defying the DCL, Charles Gordon saved his firm and alerted other companies to the idea that they could control their own destiny.

He died in December 2013. Today you can buy Girvan Single Grain: a fitting tribute to a remarkable man and his legacy.

* There was only one channel and there was no internet. Just imagine, boys and girls; whatever did people do? They watched the telly, that's what. It was a huge success.

27

Producer | W & A Gilbey Ltd
Distillery | Glen Spey, Rothes, Morayshire
Visitor Centre | No
Availability | Rare

GLEN SPEY CLENLIVET WHI

SAMPLE

Quality Castle GLEN-SPEY
soft flavoured Whisky, thoroughly
Strength 38 under proof by distilling
tested by Sykes's Hydrometer
Measure Six bottles contain approx
gallon

Bottled & Guaranteed by

CASTLE
GLEN SPEY
ROTHES

1896 Season
Pure Malt

Glen Spey
1896 Season

This little bottle tells quite a story: several, in fact.

It's a miniature of Glen Spey, a Rothes distillery that you may well never have heard of. That's because it maintains a very low profile to this day, with effectively all of the output going into the present owner's blends. But blending is why the distillery was built in the first place, which, strange as it may seem, explains the existence of this little bottle. So read on...

The first thing to note is that it's slightly larger than today's mini – around 7cl, compared to the 5cl measure that is the current standard.

Secondly, it carries the words '1896 Season' and, just under the brand name, 'Sample'. It is also described as being by W & A Gilbey – all of which is quite interesting. The distillery didn't start production until 1885*, and in October 1887 W & A Gilbey, an important London wine merchant with extensive interests in Bordeaux, bought Glen Spey from its founder James Stuart§ to secure supplies for their blends (they also owned Strathmill).

So, what the label suggests is that quite soon after they bought the distillery, samples of the make were being distributed in the trade to sell fillings to other blenders. That's quite normal today but it's fascinating to see historical evidence of the practice which has helped carry Scotch whisky to such success.

But the firm themselves remained conflicted on the question of blending. Sir Walter Gilbey himself wrote in 1904 that when 'the produce of the Patent Still is blended with a Pot Still Whisky, it is but a very poor compromise.' However, within a very few years commercial reality trumped this idealism and blends swept all before them.

Gilbey was also a firm advocate of direct firing (where the stills are heated by the direct application of flame, rather than via heating coils), insisting that only direct firing 'imparts to the Spirit the character known as empyreumatic which… is quite absent in Spirit produced by the Patent Still.' 'Empyreumatic' means 'burnt organic matter': if he tasted that I wonder if his stillman wasn't sleeping on the job.

W & A Gilbey continued independently in business until 1962 when they joined with Justerini & Brooks to form International Distillers and Vintners. Today they are part of Diageo and remembered principally for their eponymous gin.

* A visitor to the plant in 1885 remarked dolefully 'We are among those who think that the best days of distilling are numbered with the past.'
§ Who was at the same time leaseholder at The Macallan.

28

Producer
Distillery
Visitor Centre
Availability

Lost

John Smith
Glenavon, Ballindalloch, Morayshire
Yes, at today's The Glenlivet
Sold!

GLENAVON
★ ★ ★
SPECIAL LIQUEUR
WHISKY
Bottled by the Distillers

Glenavon
Special Liqueur

This little bottle – it's around the size of today's half bottle – caused rather a stir when it was sold at Bonham's in November 2006 for the then-astonishing sum of £14,850 plus buyer's premium, comfortably above the upper estimate of £10,000.

Was it authentic? If so, it is almost certainly the oldest bottle of Scotch whisky known anywhere in the world, and has been recognised as such by Guinness World Records.

At the auction, it was described as having been owned by an Irish family for generations. Though there were few details given of the exact provenance, the vendor claimed that it had been in the family house since at least the 1920s. The distillery itself was a short-lived operation in Ballindalloch, Speyside, which closed down in the 1850s and it was suggested that this was bottled by them between 1851 and 1858. There are, of course, no records remaining so, frankly, quite a lot of this is supposition.

We do know that the licensee was John Smith, who distilled in the area with his father and went on to establish the present-day site of The Glenlivet in 1859.

A number of commentators noted the high fill level, which was thought suspicious. Personally I would be inclined to give it the benefit of the doubt. Though it appeared after an earlier wave of rather dubious bottles which had given cause for concern, I imagine that a counterfeiter – having got hold of a genuinely old bottle – would have attempted to label it from a rather more fashionable distillery than the virtually unknown Glenavon.

What's more, having had a success with this, a second bottle would surely have emerged from the fraudster's lair. The fact that this is the only bottle ever seen from Glenavon, though hardly compelling evidence, does rather encourage the belief that it is genuine.

So let's wave it through. We'll accept this as both the oldest surviving bottle of Scotch whisky in the world and the sole survivor of a lost distillery. As such, it must be legendary.

But, intriguingly, no one knows where it is today.

Perhaps even more intriguing is the question of what this might fetch if it reappeared at auction. I think there's a very real chance that this could sell for well over £100,000 in the febrile atmosphere that now surrounds whisky.

I'd certainly want a seat at that sale.

29

Producer
Distillery
Visitor Centre
Availability

J & G Grant
Glenfarclas, Ballindalloch, Moraysh
Yes
Specialists

www.glenfarclas.co.uk

Glenfarclas

The Family Casks

OK, let's get the disclaimers out of the way: yes, I did write the official history of the distillery for their 175th Anniversary and, yes, they did include a copy of *101 World Whiskies* with their 21 Years Old as a gift pack for Christmas 2013*. What great taste they have.

That confessed, I still believe this extraordinary range of whiskies attains legendary status for three reasons:

Firstly, it is unique. Glenfarclas launched this in 2007, initially offering 43 different bottlings covering the years 1952 to 1994. There have been further releases since then and today the range runs until 1996. Only a strongly independent-minded, family-owned distillery could do this. No other range comes close.

Secondly, they represent exceptional value for money. In particular and by comparison to any other competitive offering, the older years are remarkably cheap. You can still find the 1953 for around £1,500. These whiskies are priced to be drunk. Glenfarclas don't spend a lot of money on advertising or elaborate packaging and that is reflected in the price. I've heard them criticised by rivals who argue that they could get a lot more for these whiskies if they just dressed them up a bit. This has, in fact, occurred to Glenfarclas and they decided not to do it as they want people to be able to enjoy their whisky. Get in quick before they change their mind, is my advice. More recent releases, such as the combination pack of 1953 Glenfarclas and Hine Cognac, have shown an alarming tendency to follow the money.

Thirdly, for the most part they are very, very good. I add that small qualifier because I can't claim to have drunk all of them, but the ones I have tried, I have generally greatly enjoyed. The older vintages remain remarkably fresh and lively.

Family-owned independent companies are now a rarity in the whisky industry, which is, for the most part, owned by global giants like Diageo, Pernod Ricard and Bacardi. One can't deny that they have brought a great deal of investment to the industry and helped build Scotch in world markets, while the previous owners – for their own good reasons – were content to take the money, but I still feel something has been lost. I show you the Family Casks and rest my case. I say again: no other range comes close.

So try one or more of the older vintages, if you can. They show the effect of quality wood and long, slow maturation in traditional warehouses.

* And may 1,000 angels sing hosannas in their name.

Producer
Distillery
Visitor Centre
Availability

William Grant & Sons Distillers Ltd
Glenfiddich, Dufftown, Morayshire
Yes
Widespread

www.glenfiddich.com

Glenfiddich
12 Years Old

Of course you know Glenfiddich. But do you really? How long is it since you tried it? So utterly ubiquitous is its familiar triangular bottle that it's easy to dismiss it.

But that would be a gross misjudgement. This whisky – well, not this one exactly, because it didn't start out life as a 12-year-old expression – can be credited with starting a revolution, and for that it is deserving of every whisky drinker's respect. Glenfiddich was the first single (or 'pure' as they used to style it) malt marketed with any intent or seriousness. And for a long time, it had the field virtually to itself. Others then jumped in and we have the mad maelstrom that we enjoy today (and which keeps me in books).

However, some people have kept faith with this brand. It's the world's best-selling single malt, for one thing, being the only brand selling more than 1 million cases annually and, for another, it claims to be 'the world's most-awarded single malt'. By this they mean that (and I quote): 'The Glenfiddich range has received more awards since 2000 than any other single malt Scotch whisky in two of the world's most prestigious competitions, the International Wine & Spirit Competition and the International Spirits Challenge.'

That seems fair enough to me. There's been a trend for everyone and his dog to start an award scheme and today there are more medals being slung about than you'll see on the chest of the average African dictator: The Midwest Whisky Olympics, for goodness sake (did they ask the International Olymic Committee? What do you think?); The International Whisky Competition (which I thought had collapsed under the weight of scornful web comment but is still soliciting entries for 2014); and, reminiscent of Baldrick's 'cunning plan', the Wizards of Whisky. I do worry that many of these are little more than 'get rich quick' schemes dreamt up by wannabe entrepreneurs: you don't have to be entirely cynical to conclude that some distillers enter them just to collect a gong and call themselves 'award-winning'.

The discerning among you will doubtless take the view that more than 50 years consistent innovation, product excellence, determined marketing in the face of many larger competitors and resolute independence qualifies for the status of a legend.

More than 12,000,000 bottles a year can't be wrong.

31

Producer William Grant & Sons Distillers Ltd
Distillery Glenfiddich, Dufftown, Morayshire
Visitor Centre Yes
Availability Extremely limited

Luxurious

www.glenfiddich.com

Glenfiddich

1937

Bottled at 64 years of age, there were only 61 bottles worth of whisky left when they came to empty the cask. At the time (2002) this was the oldest whisky ever bottled and, at the launch price of £10,000, the most expensive whisky on the market.

What I like about it is the packaging, or rather the lack of it. You'll notice it comes in the standard triangular bottle used for the Glenfiddich you can buy in your local supermarket or drinks store. OK, it's a different colour but this is a pretty modest and self-effacing approach to take, even allowing for the obligatory wooden box.

Now, in all the hype that we hear about whisky as an investment, much is made of the performance of the world's top wines, especially first-growth Bordeaux, such as Château Lafite Rothschild, Château Latour and Château Margaux. Unless I am very much mistaken, these are to be found in the same humble bottle as your everyday kitchen claret – wine you can find for less than £10 in any supermarket. The label might be a little nicer and the cork will be higher grade, but that won't add more than a few pence to the price.

So why the huge difference in price (you might easily pay over £1,000 for a bottle from a decent vintage) if the packaging costs much the same as the stuff you and I like to drink? D'oh! Because the wine is better, that's why. But with whisky it seems that incredible packaging is de rigueur, contributing many thousands of pounds to the final cost, as everyone in the distribution chain adds their percentage mark-up to the cost as it leaves the distillery.

You might think that if distillers thought their whisky worth these stratospheric prices they would have the confidence to put it in a standard bottle and let the product speak for itself. Or reduce the price by the cost of the fancy packaging. Or, and why not try this for an idea, sell the whisky in a plain package but with the option to buy the smart wrappings as an extra.

Glenfiddich eschewed the emperor's new clothes with this release and it doesn't appear to have held back the 'investment' potential. A bottle would cost you upwards of £50,000 now, if you could find one. Lucky the people who can see past the bombast and glitter.

I just wish Glenfiddich still had the courage of their convictions. Recent releases are getting more and more elaborate. I'm not sure it's really necessary.

32

Producer
Distillery
Visitor Centre
Availability

William Grant & Sons Distillers Ltd
Glenfiddich, Dufftown, Morayshire
Yes
Possibly at auction

www.glenfiddich.com

Glenfiddich
Janet Sheed Roberts Reserve

In the breathless words of Bonhams' press release: 'A rare and exclusive bottle of 55-Year-Old Glenfiddich, commemorating and celebrating the 110th birthday of Janet Sheed Roberts, the granddaughter of William Grant – founder of the Glenfiddich distillery – and the oldest person in Scotland, sold for a world record £46,850 at Bonhams Whisky auction in Edinburgh on 14 December [2011]. The previous world record for a bottle of single malt at auction was £29,700.'

That was the third of eleven bottles sold. But like taxis in the rain (you'll wait for ages and then several turn up at once), it wasn't long before a further example of this remarkable whisky set a new world record. In March 2012 a New York buyer paid $94,000 (£59,252) in aid of SHFT Initiatives, a charity improving the health of individuals, communities and the environment. In fact, all eleven bottles were sold for various charities, raising a total of more than £400,000.

But, be honest, nice though that was to know, are you that bothered? Surely, you just want to know what a £60,000 bottle of whisky tastes like. Frankly, I have no idea. But Bonhams wrote quite lyrically about it, so I have reproduced their tasting notes below: 'This precious whisky is pale gold in colour, the hue of autumn barley. On the nose, it is light and delicate with aromas of soft orange blossom and delicate violets intermingling with notes of toasted almonds and the subtlest whiff of smoke, the sweetness brought out more with a few drops of water. A perfect harmony of fruit and floral aromas, it has a surprisingly light touch of oak, incredible for a whisky that has spent so long in European wood.

'On the taste, creamy vanilla and a gentle smokiness are beautifully counterbalanced with some sweeter oak notes. A drop or two of water releases further zesty orange flavours and an incredible vibrancy. Immediately after tasting, the finish is slightly dry, but grows with time to become extremely long, lively and sweet.'

That's enough from the PR Department. By all accounts, Ms Roberts was a fine, upstanding lady whose long life is fittingly commemorated in these exceptional bottles.

33

Producer	MacDonald & Muir
Distillery	Glenmorangie, Tain, Ross-shire
Visitor Centre	Yes
Availability	Auctions and occasional specialists

Luxurious

www.glenmorangie.com

Glenmorangie
1963 Vintage

Here's a curiosity – a whisky that came back from the dead. Back in 1987 Glenmorangie broke with their established practice and released a vintage (their first) that had been finished in sherry casks (up until then they had been resolutely insisting bourbon was the only wood).

Not so very long afterwards I was working for them*. I seem to recall that there was quite a bit of stock left and one prominent UK retailer actually returned their bottles as unsaleable at £69. But that's not how the company tell it today: according to a recent press release, the 6,000 bottles were 'greeted with applause' and they now claim this to be 'the earliest known commercial bottling of a whisky that has been "wood finished"'. Maybe so, though the Balvenie Classic (which has also earned itself a place in this book) has a decent claim, as it was launched in 1982. In any event, my memory is of an experiment to 'freshen up' some over-aged casks so a touch of PR pixie dust may have been applied here. It certainly wasn't the life-changing event that they would have you believe now.

But why would there be a press release for a whisky from nearly 30 years ago? Because back then a few cases were tucked away for future celebrations. Somehow 50 bottles survived. They've now been dressed up in glitzy new packaging (silver labels and a 'time capsule' box, whatever that may be) with the price hiked up to around £1,650 and have been given a launch party with a link to Lamborghini that may strike you as a trifle spurious (drink and drive, anyone?).

But the original bottle turns up in auction from time to time and generally fetches around £700. So, given that the whisky is exactly the same, the proposition here is that you're asked to pay a cool thousand pounds for a natty box and a silver cap and label. I suppose that must work for someone.

However, I do think that we can call this 'legendary'. It was innovative, albeit rather accidentally, and it demonstrated that Glenmorangie wasn't as mono-dimensional as, up until then, it had been, so credit where it's due.

I had a bottle years ago, which I drank. I seem to remember it was rich and luxurious. Happy Days!

* Pretty briefly as it happened – the then-MD and I marched to the beat of different drums, and I was shortly drummed out!

85

34

Luxurious

Producer | MacDonald & Muir
Distillery | Glenmorangie, Tain, Ross-shire
Visitor Centre | Yes
Availability | Auctions and occasional specialists

www.glenmorangie.com (but you won't find anything about this)

Glenmorangie

Native Ross-shire

Right. Before we go any further, let's get this out of the way: this was my little baby. I dreamt it up; I wrote the copy on the unusual wrap-round label; and I pushed this through to launch, despite the scepticism of my then-colleagues, who simply didn't get it.

After I left Glenmorangie (having fallen out with the then-MD) it was pretty quickly withdrawn. So why do I think it deserves a place here?

Because this was a product ahead of its time. This, whatever anyone else claims, was the first single-cask, cask-strength single malt from a named brand – and as such it was the precursor of a flood of present day releases. Today, everyone is doing it but, believe me, in 1991 this was both controversial and radical.

Back in 1991 when I launched it, you could get Glenfarclas 105 (a vatting of several casks) and the numbered but anonymous releases from the Scotch Malt Whisky Society and a little-known bottling called 'As We Get It' (unbranded, but probably The Macallan in those days). Hard though it may be to believe, the Scotch Malt Whisky Society (SMWS, of whom more elsewhere) was something of a pariah, frowned on by the whisky establishment and regarded at best as a tiresome nuisance. For what was then Scotland's best-selling malt whisky to release a single cask, with all its glorious variability, was thought dangerously eccentric.

But I had taken some visitors round the distillery and tasted whisky direct from the cask. 'Why can't we put this in a bottle?' I asked myself. And so I made it happen and I'm still proud that I did.

So, as the very first example of something which is now commonplace, it is an important bottle. You can still find one at auction and, at around £100 or so, you can afford to do what was intended – drink it and get as close as possible to whisky straight from the cask.

It's in the nature of this product that every bottling will be different. But the aim was to showcase classic Glenmorangie – that is to say, a 10-year-old whisky matured solely in bourbon casks, preferably first fill. It captures the delicacy and refinement of this superb whisky but without any dilution of its cask-strength power.

35

Producer
Distillery
Visitor Centre
Availability

Lost

Glenmorangie
Glenmorangie, Tain, Ross-shire
Yes
Exceedingly rare

THE IMMORTAL WALTER SCOTT 1832

GLEN MORANGIE

PURE HIGHLAND MALT WHISKY

GUARANTEED TEN YEARS OLD

"My Strength is as the strength of Ten Because my 'malt' is pure." Tennyson

Glenmorangie
'Walter Scott'

What madness is this, you are asking? What has Buxton been drinking?

Well, I'll admit that I did think twice about including any minis here. But then I spoke to some collectors about their Lilliputian love affair with these tiny bottles and began to understand, if not share, the frightening intensity with which they pursue their quarry.

And this little critter is certainly highly desirable in mini-collecting circles. If not the Holy Grail of minis, it's in the top five. Dating from the 1920s the label is very different both from the classic Glenmorangie label that we all grew up with and today's more effeminate version. But variant labels are known: two further rather charming examples are illustrated in Derek Cooper's excellent *A Taste of Scotch*.

The one opposite shows a rather cavalier attitude to literary references. The gentleman with the red waistcoat is carrying a stone carved to honour Sir Walter Scott and, one presumes, has emptied the bottle at his feet (which is most assuredly not a miniature) in acknowledgement of the cod reference to Tennyson's 'Sir Galahad'*.

At one time Glenmorangie seemed slightly obsessed with Scott. He appears on the two labels illustrated by Derek Cooper and the stone, so manfully borne aloft here, is not just any stone. No, this is the glacial erratic which you may find to this day by the west side of the A9, just north of the distillery. It is inscribed in honour of Sir Walter Scott, reputedly by a mason working on a nearby bridge who admired the great man's writings. It's rather a fine piece of work and well worth stopping to admire. The distillery was evidently greatly taken by it at one time: perhaps they should adopt it.

This miniature is believed to be extremely rare. Glenmorangie itself enjoys a legendary status as one of the first single malts to be promoted outside of Scotland and, indeed, I've included some other references to the brand elsewhere in this book. But should you ever see one of these tiny bottles for sale be sure to swoop on it. Even if you don't want it, don't have a heart of stone: somewhere a slightly obsessed mini collector yearns for it.

Strange as it may seem, I wasn't allowed to open it.

* As any schoolboy in the 1920s would have known, it was Sir Galahad's *heart* that was pure, not his malt. You've got to admit, it's a real rib-tickler.

36

Producer
Distillery
Visitor Centre

Availability

James Worts
Gooderham & Worts, Toronto, Cana
Now developed as The Distillery
District
Random sightings

www.distilleryheritage.com

Gooderham & Worts

We can't let the legends of various haunted distilleries pass by unnoticed. But which one should we include here? Any abandoned distillery seems to have a ghostly, haunted air. If you will excuse the inevitable but very poor pun, there are restless spirits there.

Quite a number of distilleries have ghosts: several previous owners are said to roam Kilbeggan in Ireland; Glen Scotia and Glenkinchie are among Scotland's allegedly haunted distilleries; and Buffalo Trace in Kentucky boasts 27 different spectral presences*.

But the old Gooderham & Worts distillery in Toronto is slightly different. Founded in 1831 by James Worts§ as a mill, it didn't actually start distilling until six years later but, by the second half of the 19th century, was producing over 2.1 million gallons (about 9.5 million litres) annually, making it one of the largest distilleries in the world◦.

It was, in its day, a legendary producer and of massive importance to the Canadian market. Gooderham & Worts' whisky was even exported to Liverpool and London.

Poor James Worts didn't live to see any of this. In 1834 his wife died in childbirth and the unfortunate man is said to have committed suicide by drowning himself in the well of their prominent windmill. His ghost remained at peace until 1923 when the distilling business, then hard hit by the Temperance movement and the effects of Prohibition, was sold by the family. The new owner, Harry C. Hatch, was less fastidious about his customers and sales to middlemen with questionable connections over the border in the USA saved the firm.

But the soul of James Worts appears to have been unsettled by these unsavoury associations and reports of mysterious noises, bizarre and unexplained events (such as doors that opened and shut and lights than flickered on and off without apparent cause) duly began. Visitors and workers alike were disturbed by these manifestations. Though the ghost seems to have been essentially benign, a witness in 2005 claimed to have seen it walk through a door.

Spooky!

But we'll have no jokes here about body in the whisky. That would leave a bad taste in your mouth.

* Is it just me, or is that a trifle over the top? One could excuse one or two ghosts but 27 just seems greedy.
§ Now do you believe in nominative determinism?
◦ Some sources say it was the largest, though the giant Dublin distillers must have run it close.

37

Producer Gordon & MacPhail
Distillery n/a
Visitor Centre Retail shop, South Street, Elgin, Morayshire
Availability Widespread

www.gordonandmacphail.com

Gordon & MacPhail

Can a shop be a whisky legend? In this case, I think so – but Gordon & MacPhail are much, much more than their famous shop in South Street, Elgin.

The firm was established in 1895 as 'Family Grocers, Tea, Wine & Spirit Merchants'. It was a propitious moment: there was a major whisky boom going on and Speyside was benefitting from it, with a general rise in prosperity. Quite a number of famous whisky firms started in this way and we may include in their number: Gloags of Perth (The Famous Grouse); Johnnie Walker; Chivas Brothers; Buchanan's; Dewar's; and Graham Brothers (Black Bottle), among many others.

But while most have either been acquired by a major group and lost touch with their roots or disappeared entirely, Gordon & MacPhail have gone from strength to strength. The shop continues to this day and is a delight and a pleasure to visit. But the firm now does so much more: commissioning new fillings; bottling an extensive range of whiskies under various labels; wholesaling wines and spirits (many a pub and hotel rely on them); and, since 1993 when they acquired and set about refurbishing Benromach, distilling in their own right.

Continuity of family ownership has been critical to this. Since the firm passed to John Urquhart in 1915 it has been controlled by his descendants. As good, prudent Scots they have not absented themselves to live on the profits but have managed the business directly and personally, right through to the fourth generation.

For many years, they were one of the very few places where it was possible to buy single malt whisky. Along with Milroys of Soho it may be said that they kept the flame of self whiskies burning against a sea of blends. For this alone they should be legends but, in addition, they are able to release whiskies of extraordinary age and quality – often far older than the parent distillery – because they have been buying new fillings almost from the start for their broking business.

Their ultimate range is known as the Generations. It includes two whiskies of 70 years old (Mortlach and The Glenlivet) and an outstanding 60-year-old Glen Grant, bottled in 2012 to mark the 60th anniversary of HM Queen Elizabeth II's accession to the throne.

But you don't have to pay the many thousands of pounds these cost to experience the G&M legend: anything with their name on the label is good. Because, back in 1895 they promised customers 'the utmost satisfaction'. They are still delivering.

38

Producer
Distillery
Visitor Centre

Availability

Irish Distillers Ltd
Midleton, Cork, Ireland
Retail shop at the CHQ Building,
Dublin
Specialists

www.mitchellandson.com

Green Spot

This is a living legend – a coelacanth of whisky. Let's salute Mitchell's of Dublin, a traditional wine merchant of the old school who, when all others had abandoned the pot still legacy of Irish whiskey, kept the flame burning. A flickering flame, it's true, because at the nadir of its fortunes a mere 500 cases a year were being produced and there remained a constant threat that Irish Distillers would decide that such tiny volumes were not worth the effort, especially considering the scale of their Midleton distillery operations.

Fortunately a small but well-informed group of enthusiasts continued to buy this wonderful whiskey from Mitchell's, despite packaging that until its recent revamp was decidedly downbeat (pay attention marketing types: this suggests that some people do at least care more about what's in the bottle than how it looks on the shelf). This was the last of an all-but-forgotten style – the merchant's bottling. At one time, most independent wine and spirit merchants would have had their own whiskey – with the slow demise of Irish whiskey that continued until very recently, almost all of these had been lost. Even Mitchell's had trimmed the range from Blue, Red and Yellow Spot to just the Green.

And then its fortunes changed. Irish Distillers (IDL), sensing the success of their Redbreast brand and seeing the interest and growing sales of single malt Scotch, determined that Irish pot still whiskey was overdue a revival. So, to the acclaim of whiskey lovers, they worked with Mitchell's to re-launch Yellow Spot in May 2012 as a 12-year-old and gave both styles a packaging makeover. I'll grudgingly admit that it looks rather smart.

Along with this, IDL have launched their own revivalist pot still whiskies such as the Power's John's Lane Edition and added a 21-year-old to Redbreast. Irish distilling is generally storming back into life and once again representing real competition in global whisky markets. And a good thing it is, too.

If you visit Dublin, you should try and visit Mitchell's and buy your bottle there. It's more widely available than ever and growing in popularity, but it is only fitting that – if you can – you go to the source and reward their patience and persistence.

Just to whet your appetite a little, I'd describe this as a very distinctive whiskey with a lovely waxy, oily, mouth-coating impact. The nose suggests greengage jam and the taste gives honey, mint, cloves, wood notes and lots of spice.

39

Producer	Hannis Distilling Co.
Distillery	Hannisville, Pennslyvania, USA
Visitor Centre	No
Availability	Online

www.finestandrarest.com

Hannisville Rye

This is, without doubt, the oldest spirit – Armagnac included – that I have ever drunk. This fact alone would make it memorable. That it is also extraordinarily enjoyable is almost too much.

I obtained a 20cl sample bottle from a remarkable website FinestandRarest.com which specialises in finding really old bottles of absinthe and other spirits. If you're lucky, they may have some left. If so, I urge you to purchase without delay.

There was once a great distilling industry in the state of Pennsylvania, little of which survived Prohibition. Hannis Distilling was one of those companies but I can't really do more than reprint the story of this whiskey, as told by the vendors:

The Hannisville Rye you purchased has been in my family since 1913 if not longer. Family lore has it that the Hannisville Rye was distilled in 1863, was held in oak barrels for 50 years or until 1913 when it was put into the carboys now in your possession. The rye was purchased by my great-great grandfather, John Welsh of Philadelphia who had served as Ambassador to the Court of Saint James, 1877-1879*.

The carboys you have were initially stored at the Merchants Cold Storage and Warehouse Co. of Providence, RI... then moved to my great-father's summer home, Shadow Farm in Wakefield, RI, where they remained until 1985, when at my grandmother's death they were moved to my parent's home in Saunderstown, RI. In 2003 the carboys came into my possession at my mother's passing. For the first time in almost 100 years the Hannisville Rye has passed from my family.

So – if the story is to be believed and I have no reason to doubt it – this is 150 years old or, as it was put into glass in 1913, strictly speaking it is a 100-year-old sample of 50-year-old rye. Either way, it's an extraordinary pre-Prohibition survival.

I know I really should get out more, but drinking this was quite a moving and emotional experience[§].

This book isn't really about tasting notes (you can find lots of books and websites that do that really well) but I thought this exceptionally long-lived survivor deserved one:

Colour: A rich, deep, burnished gold.

Aroma: Overpoweringly intense and complex with citrus fruits, spice, honey, caramel, liquorice and vanilla.

Palate: All of the above present in rich abundance, with mint, dry ash and wax all added. Remarkable!

* In other words, he was the US Ambassador to Great Britain.
[§] OK, I'll admit it. I haven't quite finished all of the 20cl. It seemed sacrilegious to pour the very last drops.

40

Producer — Suntory
Distillery — n/a – this is a blend
Visitor Centre — Yes – at Yamazaki and Hakushu distilleries
Availability — Specialists

www.suntory.com

Hibiki

This is what Suntory themselves have to say about Hibiki. Grip the sides of your chair firmly because, even by the standards of overblown hyperbole adopted by the whisky industry's PR spinmeisters, this is pretty rich:

The legendary Hibiki represents true harmony. The enigma of perfection, the paragon of the art of whisky and the art of Japan's artisans.

Hibiki, meaning resonance in Japanese, speaks to the soul and emotions of the most discerning whisky lover. Hibiki resonates from nature, and all the subtleties found from the twenty-four seasons of the old Japanese lunar calendar. Numerous types of pure single malt whiskies ageing in various types of casks, including Mizunara, a very rare Japanese oak, all combine to create a full orchestra of flavors and aromas. Seductive, blossoming and enigmatic, Hibiki celebrates the unrivalled art of blending, fine craftsmanship, and sense of luxury of the House.

You've got to agree that's something. But, actually, this is very fine whisky. It's perhaps rather a cliché now in enlightened whisky circles to praise Japanese whisky (far better to pick something obscure from Venezuela, the more outré the better, so as to impress with your arcane knowledge) but the reputation of Japanese whisky, which not so long ago wasn't that high, was built by products like this.

The various expressions, which run to a 30-year-old version if your pocket can stand it (expect to pay anything up to £900 for a bottle), have collected a hatful of medals, too tedious to recite here, from all the major award schemes that matter. Rightly so, for this is a superb whisky which is justly deserving of the tag 'legendary' and all the gongs it has collected. The website copy may be over the top and the bottle a little feminine for some tastes, but just wait until you get it open.

Not for nothing has the 30-year-old style been called the 'World's Best Blended Whisky'. Personally I don't really subscribe to this 'world's best' malarkey, believing such a sweeping judgment to be both simplistic and reductionist of such a majestically complex spirit as whisky, where subjective personal preference must play a role, but I do see what they are getting at as it is really quite sublime. Fortunately, though it's not cheap, you should be able to find some

It's worth the effort to experience its complexity, great allure and sustained crescendo of a finish.

41

Producer
Distillery
Visitor Centre
Availability

Highland Distillers
Highland Park, Kirkwall, Orkney
Yes
Specialists

www.highlandpark.co.uk

Highland Park
50 Years Old

I have a very great fondness for Orkney and for Highland Park. It's one of my favourite distilleries and a whisky that I love for its apparent ability to fit appropriately into almost any occasion.

All the range is good but if you feel like splashing some serious cash then there are two 50-year-old expressions available to you. The first was distilled in 1902 (imagine that!) and was bottled by Berry Bros. & Rudd in 1952. The second was released by the distillery itself in 2010.

Technically, the BB&R bottling is not legally whisky, as bottles were tested by Oxford University and shown to be very slightly under-strength at 39.8% abv*. I wouldn't turn it down on those grounds, though. The 2010 release comes in at 44.8%, so that's all right then.

Comparing the two bottles (the bottles, not the contents) tells you something about how whisky has changed in the last 60 years. The 1952 bottling is in, well, a standard tall round bottle with a paper label. And that's it.

The latest release, however, comes in a special bottle, itself encased in a filigree of silver created by Scottish artist Maeve Gillies, designed to remind you of strands of seaweed. It is then placed in a custom-made oak box with a porthole through which you glimpse the bottle. If you drink enough of the whisky (and what's stopping you tearing right into it?) you will glimpse a rose window design on the rear of the sandstone Highland Park logo.

All this comes at a cost, though. While you can still find the last few of the Berry Bros.' bottles in specialists at around £7,500, the 'new' 50 Years Old was launched at £10,000 and has appreciated since. If you can't find a bottle, you'll have to wait until 2014 for the next release.

All this is wonderful stuff and Highland Park is truly a very special and wonderful place. I do have one slight concern, however, and that is the number and pace of recent 'collectable' releases. It would be easy to overestimate the demand for this type of thing and – it may just be me – the latest editions based on Norse Gods seem a trifle contrived. Probably is me; they seem to sell we'll enough.

They aren't Gods but, back in 1883, the King of Denmark and his pal the Russian Emperor determined Highland Park's whisky 'the finest they had ever tasted'. Who am I to disagree?

* Whisky is now required by law to have a minimum strength of 40% abv.

42

Producer
Distillery
Visitor Centre
Availability

Luxury Beverage Company
Unknown
No
Who knows?

Isabella's Islay

Perhaps an English crystal decanter, coated in white gold and then studded with 8,500 white diamonds and almost 300 rubies, containing a 'Very Old Single Malt cask strength Islay whisky' (sic) is your thing. Perhaps you have a spare $6.2 million (that's nearly £4 million) lying around and like a peaty dram of an evening.

Or perhaps – like me – you consider this so vulgar, ostentatious and lacking in any sort of taste that it becomes surreally amusing. So grotesque, in fact, that when I first saw it launched I assumed it was an April Fool. But it was May 2011 when this burst into the consciousness of an underwhelmed public, courtesy of some gullible hacks who latched on to the story of 'the world's most expensive whisky'. The Macallan had just sold their Macallan Cire Perdue (see separate entry) and there was much over-excited hype about the stratospheric price of whisky. Into this over-heated arena entered the previously unknown Luxury Beverage Company with this astonishing offering.

Surely no one would buy this, I wondered, but made a note to check it out for this book. Any whisky selling for $6.2m would surely be legendary, no matter how crass the packaging. At the time, The Whisky Exchange blog had some fun at the expense of Isabella's Islay only to be contacted by the irate proprietor of the company, which suggests that it really was a live project at least for a while.

The website is still active (at the time of writing), but an online check at Companies House had the Luxury Beverage Company as 'dissolved' in January 2013. It only appears to have lasted a month over two years and didn't return any accounts. Luxury Beverage was based in a block of small office suites in Didsbury, a suburb of Manchester, with neighbours including Pottery from Poland Ltd, Ace Gas Services and Didsbury Cellar Conversions Ltd, who I suppose might be handy if you needed somewhere to keep your decanter.

I did find an email for the person said to be behind the project but – as we go to press – I haven't had a reply. I have no idea what whisky was going to be housed in this extraordinary object and, who knows, perhaps I dreamt all this up anyway?

Isabella's Islay – legendary or mythical? You decide.

And who, for that matter, is or was Isabella? I believe we should be told.

43

Producer
Distillery
Visitor Centre

Availability

Brown-Forman Corporation
Lynchburg, Tennessee, USA
Yes – the whole town of Lynchburg
given over to it
Widespread

www.jackdaniels.com

Jack Daniels

Not many American whiskies make it into this record of whisky greatness (take a look at the entry for Jim Beam if you want to know why) but this behemoth of global marketing can't be ignored. It is, quite simply, an American icon with some of the most distinctive packaging anywhere.

I started to list its appearances in popular culture but after counting at least 16 films, including *Animal House*, *The Shining*, *Scent of a Woman* and so on, and noting that Frank Sinatra was – allegedly – buried along with a bottle (it certainly appeared on his concert riders), I gave up trying to record all the songs and movies in which it appears. I concluded that it is, quite simply, a shorthand way of establishing a character's All American, rock 'n' roll*, good old boy personality. And what's wrong with that?

Assisted by great advertising, distinguished for its consistency in a world where brand managers change places faster than Premier League footballers move teams, and by loyal consumers who simply order 'Jack', oblivious to the fact that this is Tennessee whiskey they're slugging back, not the bourbon many imagine it to be, this has become a global phenomenon.

Often drunk with Coca Cola and considerable quantities of ice, to the detriment of the finer points of its filtration through sugar maple charcoal, this can hardly be considered a connoisseur's whiskey, though the brand offers premium expressions for those ready to pay a few dollars more.

The massive distillery operates a successful visitor centre in its home town of Lynchburg which, as often commented upon, is located in a 'dry' county, though the distillery has a special waiver allowing them to sell you a bottle. A substantial tourist economy has sprung up to service the many visitors, but don't let that put you off. It may be moderated and curated within an inch of its life, with suspiciously folksy guides, but it's still fun.

The origin of the 'Old No. 7' designation is fiercely disputed. What is more rarely publicised is that the original recipe may have been created by a herbalist from Llanelli and Mr Jack may have been taught the art of distilling by a slave named Nearest Green.

May have been.

* There's a classic 1972 shot by photographer Jim Marshall, *Mike Jagger Backstage with Jack Daniels Bottle* in which the cricket-loving rock god caresses a bottle. From his wilder period.

44

Living

Producer	Irish Distillers Ltd
Distillery	Midleton, Cork, Ireland
Visitor Centre	Yes
Availability	Widespread

www.jamesonwhiskey.com

Jameson
Limited Reserve 18 Years Old

As you would expect, Jameson don't exactly highlight the fact that their great Dublin distillery was founded by a Scotsman, John Stein of Kennetpans, and that it wasn't until 1805 that the original John Jameson took charge. Of course, southern Ireland was part of Great Britain at the time and it wasn't all that unusual for entrepreneurial and enterprising individuals to try and make their fortune in Dublin, a major commercial centre.

But it was the Jameson family who expanded the distillery and made it, in its day, one of the largest in the world. When Alfred Barnard, arguably the world's first whisky journalist, visited there around 1886, it occupied a site of 'upwards of five acres of ground' and produced about 1 million gallons annually. That would be a good-sized distillery even today.

To cut a long and tangled story very short, Irish whiskey went into a severe decline after that and in 1966 John Jameson merged with Cork Distillers and John Powers to form Irish Distillers Ltd (IDL). A new, multi-functional distillery was built at Midleton near Cork, adjoining the old one, now a tourist attraction. All of Dublin's historic distilleries were closed. The Jameson brand was then acquired by the French drinks conglomerate Pernod Ricard in 1988, when it bought Irish Distillers.

Today they sell well over 3 million cases a year, making Jameson the number one Irish whiskey in the world. Based on recent double-digit growth and bullish projections, the distillery has recently been extensively expanded (including, I was pleased to see, an archive) and the company plans to increase greatly its share of world markets.

But that's not why it's here. Apart from publishing the two most beautiful whisky books ever, bar none*, Jameson has become almost a universal symbol of Irishness. It certainly wraps itself in the green of the emerald isle in its marketing. But for media types, a glass of Jameson is a guaranteed shorthand way of establishing the identity of your characters. More worryingly for the brand, perhaps, is that it was also consumed in prodigious quantities and in a less than discriminating manner by Detective Jimmy McNulty and friends in *The Wire*.

I'm very partial to the Limited Reserve 18 Years Old. I was first served it by Barry Crockett, IDL's veteran Master Distiller, and that man is a legend (not least because he was born on site).

I expect it was a big day for him as well.

* *The History of a Great House* and *Elixir of Life*, both illustrated by Harry Clarke and published in the 1920s. They are rare, expensive and very, very lovely.

45

Producer
Distillery
Visitor Centre
Availability

Living

Beam Global Spirits & Wine, Inc.
Clermont, Kentucky, USA
Yes
Widespread

www.jimbeam.com

Jim Beam
White Label

There are relatively few American whiskies in this book for the very good reason that a) relatively few American whiskies make it out of the USA in anything other than tiny numbers and b) I'm really not qualified to comment with any great authority on what constitutes legendary in the context of that market*.

But this is a genuine, bona fide legend. First established in 1795, the company has passed through a number of hands, survived Prohibition and the slow decline of bourbon at the hands of vodka, only to come storming back in the 21st century. Whatever else it is, it's a survivor.

There are, no doubt, better bourbons than the standard White Label; though, in fairness, it enjoys four years of barrel maturation, which is more than many everyday types of bourbon. Beyond that, Beam themselves offer superior Black and Devil's Cut versions and two flavoured styles for those who like that kind of thing.

Quite what the late Booker Noe, Beam family descendant, Master Distiller, creator of the first small batch bourbons and father of the present day Fred Noe III, would make of a bourbon flavoured with black cherry is anyone's guess but so powerful is the Beam/Noe distilling lineage that it can be linked to more than 60 other whiskey brands. They are American distilling royalty and Jim Beam White Label is their signature product.

It's been advertised by Sean Connery and Leonardo DiCaprio, appeared in films such as *Talladega Nights: The Ballad of Ricky Bobby* and *The Final Destination*§, and spawned a line of spin-off products, such as marinated meats and even a burger.

Today the parent company Beam Inc. is viewed by analysts as a takeover target for the likes of Diageo, Pernod Ricard or even Bacardi. One of the plums they would be seeking to acquire would be this iconic American original: today it is the top-selling bourbon in more than 100 countries and one of the very few global US whiskey brands, giving it a virtually unique status.

Stop Press – that was prophetic! As this book goes to press, Suntory of Japan have just announced a takeover bid, agreed by the Beam Board of Directors, to acquire the business. It will cost them some $16 billion. If anyone doubted the significance of Japan as a distilling nation, this should make them think again.

* As you've paid good money for these ramblings (thank you), I think you're entitled to some honesty.
§ I'm sure I've missed a few; write in if you must.

Producer
Distillery
Visitor Centre
Availability

Diageo
n/a – this is a blend
Yes – Cardhu Distillery, Speyside
Everywhere

EXTRA SPECIAL
Old Highland Whisky
JOHN WALKER & SONS, KILMARNOCK
(REGISTERED)
PRODUCE OF SCOTLAND

GUARANTEED
OVER
12 YEARS OLD

www.johnniewalker.com

Johnnie Walker
Black Label

What's such a ubiquitous whisky doing here, you might reasonably ask? And why have you used such a horrid picture?

Well, sorry about the picture but the bottle in it is more than 100 years old so it may be excused. Look at it closely – it's square, with a slanted label and the contents are 'guaranteed over 12 years old'. Remind you of anything?

It's the precursor to today's Johnnie Walker Black Label, of course, the best-selling premium whisky in the world and a tangible and undying link to whisky's history.

The Diageo blenders have the original blending book used by Alexander Walker and they remain true to his principles of blending, using 'blocks' of whisky, which offer distinct flavour character to deliver the final taste, bottle after bottle after bottle. It's an impressive and admirable achievement.

And, I'm happy to say, it's an achievement recognised by their peers in the industry. When I was researching the first book in the 101 series*, I asked a number of people in the industry to nominate their three 'Desert Island Drams'. Time and again they picked Black Label, which is potent testimony to the high regard in which it is held.

Rightly so, as this is a consummate blend, carrying the distinctive smoky taste that is the signature of all Walker blends and which goes right back to the product's origins on the West Coast of Scotland. A great number of Walker variants have been introduced since this was first seen but it remains the reference point for the blenders. As such, it offers unrivalled continuity and value in a world of change.

This is the kind of product that the future of Scotch whisky will be built on, and, in our Western bubble of comparative luxury and privilege, let's not forget that for many people around the world a 12–year-old whisky, especially one with this heritage and history, represents their pinnacle of aspiration, success and indulgence.

So, while it's easy to sneer at a bottle you see in all the gin joints in all the towns in all the world, it didn't get there by accident. In short, think yourself lucky.

* 101 Whiskies to Try Before You Die – a new and revised edition of arguably the finest book on whisky in the entire history of global civilisation is available from all good bookshops and major internet retailers. Don't let me detain you further; I'll be here when you get back.

47

Luxurious

Producer	Diageo
Distillery	n/a – this is a blend
Visitor Centre	Yes – Cardhu Distillery, Speyside
Availability	By invitation – or you could try aski

www.johnniewalker.com

Johnnie Walker

Diamond Jubilee

As you may have gathered, I'm not generally impressed by whiskies the point of which is – in the main – the price. But, as I don't object to people spending their own money as they see fit (daft as some of their purchases may seem) and I understand why a brand owner would want to take advantage of this sudden craze for very, very expensive whisky, you might reasonably ask: what's the problem?

The problem, of course, is that it leads to an upward drift in the price of all whiskies, as one brand follows another and the humble drinker not possessed of the riches of a bloated Russian plutocrat regularly ends up paying more for their everyday dram. If you don't believe me, try checking what your favourite tipple cost five years ago.

However, we're going to make an exception here* as Diageo have pledged all the profit from this exercise to the Queen Elizabeth Scholarship Trust to 'enable traditional craftsmanship to flourish in Britain'. It's OK by me if the world's multi-millionaires pay for that.

And one can't deny this is an extraordinary *thing*. I went to see one at Hamilton & Inches, an upmarket Edinburgh jeweller who did the silver work, and it is a mighty fine and impressive object, right down to its own huge flight case. I can recall being packed off to school for a whole term with a trunk smaller than that.

The Diamond Jubilee release commemorates the 60th anniversary of Queen Elizabeth II's accession to the British throne. Predictably, there was a rash of 'limited edition' whisky trying to cash in on the occasion – this, I think, is one of the more tasteful and elegant offerings. In its own way it could even be described as restrained.

Naturally, there were 60 of them, which might seem ambitious. However, they have sold well and, as we go to print, there are only a few left – and you have to convince Diageo that you're worthy before they'll sell you one. Rules me out then.

I did actually get to try this but under conditions of such quasi-religious solemnity and in such an absurdly small amount that I can't really recall very much about it. I seem to remember it was very nice. Sorry if you were expecting more.

* If you bought *101 World Whiskies to Try Before You Die* you'll remember this was my 102nd Bonus Whisky. Remarkable value when you come to think of it (the book, I mean, obviously).

48

Producer
Distillery
Visitor Centre
Availability

Legend

Diageo
n/a – this is a blend
Yes – Cardhu Distillery, Speyside
Impossible (unless you're a Director of Diageo)

www.johnniewalker.com

Johnnie Walker
The Director's Blend Series

Yum! Look at these lovely bottles. Don't they just tease and tantalise in their handsome party clothes? Aren't they just begging to be cracked open and shared? You can almost smell their enticing aromas, taste their rich, warming flavours.

But you can't have them. Unless, that is, you happen to be one of the '*high heid yins*' (as they say in Scotland) at Diageo or a very special friend of Johnnie Walker, and then you might, if you are very lucky, find one in your Christmas stocking*. They produce just 500 bottles each year (they're counted very carefully) and 2013 was the last in the six-year series, showcasing the six key building blocks of the Walker blend.

It's a variation on the tradition of exclusive private bottlings for the industry's top dogs, which aims to showcase different aspects of the Johnnie Walker blend character. Think of it as an educational exercise.

Being serious for a moment, these one-off editions are an exploration of the Walker house style and its 'building blocks'. They were never intended for commercial release because, by their very nature, they are very single-minded in style.

In 2008, for example, the blend highlighted the role of aged grain whisky and in 2009 the peat, wind and salty air evident in Scotland's West Coast distilleries dominated. The 2012 release showcases fruity Highland malts. Each is distinctly different and deliberately emphasises one characteristic of the Walker cardinal elements, so it is, as I say, unbalanced but never one-dimensional.

Just occasionally, a single bottle appears on the auction scene – as if by magic. That's a little naughty of the recipient. However, a complete collection was offered for sale at the 2013 Distillers' Charity Auction, donated by Diageo. So far as I'm aware, this is the one and only time that all six bottles have been available for sale. The collection fetched £23,000 but may subsequently be offered by a major retailer, unless they decide to keep it for exhibition purposes.

But, guess what? You might think that an exclusive blend of Johnnie Walker, reserved for the company's directors and valued partners would be one of the finest whiskies you could drink. In a curious way, you would be wrong. The Johnnie Walker Director's Blend is remarkable whisky, certainly, but it's deliberately unbalanced – almost the antithesis of the perfect blend. And it changes every year, when blends generally prize themselves on consistency. So try not to be too disappointed that you won't be getting any.

* Despite leaving out LOTS of mince pies, I'm still waiting.

49

Producer
Distillery

Visitor Centre

Availability

Luxurious

The Number One Drinks Company
Karuizawa Distillery, Kitasakugun,
Nagano, Japan
No – the distillery has been
demolished
Possibly at auction

一九六四年蒸溜

軽井沢

樽番子三六〇三

www.one-drinks.com

Karuizawa

1964

The Number One Drinks Company was established in August 2006 by Marcin Miller, a former publisher of *Whisky Magazine*, and his business partner in Japan, David Croll, to import and distribute some of Japan's finest whiskies for the delectation of European single malt enthusiasts.

Rather shrewdly they obtained exclusive worldwide distribution rights for Chichibu, Hanyu and Karuizawa distilleries which, I am assured, was a somewhat tortuous negotiation and something of a labour of love. However, with the 143 bottles of this 1964 distillation selling out quickly in Poland (explanation follows) at £9,000 each, there was presumably a profit in there somewhere.

Actually, it was soon followed by a mere 41 bottles of an even older Karuizawa 1960 at £12,500 but that did come in a very lovely box with its own individual and different antique *netsuke* carving. These are changed days for Japanese whiskies which are rapidly gaining an enthusiastic following.

These are among the oldest Japanese whiskies ever released, if not the oldest, and certainly among the most expensive. For me, they mark the point at which Japanese whisky attained real cult status among whisky's chattering classes (though the cognoscenti had been quietly enjoying them for some years previously). As such they deserve legendary status.

So why pick the 1964 over its older brother? Well, not to put too fine a point on it, because I have tried the former but not the latter.

And Poland? It's not where you would expect groundbreaking whiskies to be released. But Marcin Miller has Polish roots and so was completely at ease working with the Warsaw based firm of Wealth Solutions who have begun to offer rare and exclusive whiskies to their exclusive client base. The fact that they had successfully released a superb* Glenfarclas cask from 1953 didn't hurt either.

It's not clear yet whether these Polish connoisseurs are collecting this whisky, drinking it or, perish the thought, buying it as an investment. If that's their goal, presumably they will have been less than impressed by the bottle sold in October 2013 by Bonhams, New York, for a mere (!) $7,140, including buyer's premium. At rather less than half the retail price, it represents a pretty short haircut for one distressed vendor. If not distressed before consigning the bottle, we may presume that he or she certainly was at the hammer's fall.

* Declaration of Interest (for pedants): As you already know if you care about such matters, I was involved with the Glenfarclas release. There, happy now?

50

Producer
Distillery

Visitor Centre

Availability

Lost

Stein and Haig families
Kennetpans and Kilbagie,
Kennetpans, Clackmannanshire
No, but you are free to take a look
at what remains
Long gone

www.kennetpans.info

Kennetpans and Kilbagie

We're stepping back now to the late 18th century when Kennetpans and Kilbagie were flourishing mightily: 'It is difficult to overestimate the importance of Kennetpans Distillery. The site is of great importance to the industrial archaeological heritage of Scotland. It would be nothing short of a tragedy if the site was left to vanish.' So says Charles MacLean – and he can almost remember the distilleries working!*

And I wrote: 'The historical significance of Kennetpans to the history of distilling, even if little appreciated, can hardly be overstated. This is the crucible in which the modern Scotch whisky industry was formed.'

All this, and much, much more can be found on the website of the Kennetpans Trust, a body formed to preserve what remains of the Kennetpans and Kilbagie distilleries. This is a labour of love for Bryan Frew and his wife who own the site. I shudder to think of the hours of unpaid and sadly largely unappreciated work that has gone on so far and the immense task that remains ahead of them.

The ruins may be found near the Kincardine Bridge, on the upper reaches of the Forth, close to Stirling and Alloa. There the Stein and Haig families founded Scotland's – indeed the world's – first industrial distilleries. In terms of its importance to whisky, this location is worth ten of Lindores Abbey, where you will recall Friar John Cor and his eight bolls resided.

At least £1 million is needed to fund the basic restoration of the site and the stabilisation of the buildings, which remain in a remarkable state of preservation. It is probable, however, that if prompt action isn't taken more will be lost in the next 20 years than in the past 200.

Kennetpans and its sister distillery at Kilbagie really are of great importance. They may be little known but that does not diminish their significance. If any part of Scotland's distilling history, indeed its whole industrial legacy, deserves to be saved this is surely it. If that isn't a legend I don't know what is.

Having said that, in all probability the whisky they produced wasn't all that nice. Most was intended to be shipped to England for rectification into gin.

Writing in 1788 Robert Burns described whisky of this type as 'a most rascally liquor; and by consequence, only drunk by the most rascally part of the inhabitants.' So I wouldn't bother to fire up the Tardis just yet.

51

Producer   William Whiteley & Co
Distillery   n/a – this is a blend
Visitor Centre   No
Availability   Auctions

King's Ransom

I don't imagine that you've heard of this; you've probably never seen a bottle and you probably wouldn't give it a second glance if you did, dismissing it as a not especially interesting blend of indeterminate vintage. But read on.

If you were so rash as to bid for the occasional bottle that appears in auction you're unlikely to have to part with more than £50. However, for that relatively modest sum, you would have acquired an interesting and colourful part of whisky's history; a link to one of the industry's more buccaneering characters; a whisky that sank with the SS *Politician*; and a distillery bought – allegedly – with Mafia money.

King's Ransom was the 1928 creation of William Whiteley, a faintly disreputable though evidently charming salesman and discharged bankrupt. Though already possessed of a chequered career, he went on to own Edradour Distillery in Pitlochry and build King's Ransom into a successful premium blend in the USA, largely assisted by Mafia don Frank Costello (successor to Charles 'Lucky' Luciano as the 'Boss of Bosses').

Whiteley's raffish charm, 'direct' business methods and generally spivvish* behaviour would most certainly be frowned on today by the whisky establishment; such figures have been largely written out of whisky's history but they played a not insignificant part in the development of the drinks industry in the first half of the last century – Whiteley was not alone in his flexible approach to business ethics.

Prior to the purchase of Edradour by Pernod's Clan Campbell in 1982, King's Ransom was the company's leading blend. For a time, certainly pre-WW2, it was reputedly the most expensive whisky in the world, served at top hotels and enjoyed by royalty, celebrities and an affluent clientele who appreciated its stylish packaging, unusually lavish for the period. Whiteley styled himself the 'Dean of Distillers', though in truth his skill was as a consummate salesman.

He sold his interests in the brand and Edradour in 1938 to Irving Haim, an associate of Frank Costello, who may have put up some of the finance. The Haim family eventually sold out to an international consortium who sold to Pernod Ricard.

Perhaps embarrassed by the brand's associations, or possibly to give priority to their own brands, Pernod phased out King's Ransom in the 1980s, thus bringing an end to a fascinating chapter that provides a vivid contrast to today's somewhat sanitised official version of whisky's history.

* Spiv – for younger readers – a seedy and underhand sharp trader, possibly with criminal connections.

52

Producer
Distillery
Visitor Centre
Availability

The Distillers' Company Ltd
Kirkliston, nr Edinburgh
No
In your dreams

Kirkliston

What do we know about Kirkliston? Well, not a lot in truth, yet this was once one of the most important distilleries in Scotland. It was one of the six original founders of The Distillers' Company Ltd (precursor to today's Diageo).

Back in 1887 in his wonderfully lyrical account of all the United Kingdom's whisky distilleries, Alfred Barnard devoted four pages to it. Four! With two illustrations. He gave The Macallan seven lines, Port Ellen got one page, and The Glenlivet managed three and two full page pictures.

At the time, while The Macallan was making just 40,000 gallons of spirit annually, Port Ellen 140,000 and The Glenlivet 200,000, Kirkliston was making 700,000 gallons of malt and grain and, according to Barnard, it enjoyed 'a good reputation in the market'.

Even earlier in its history, the Stein family (of Kennetpans fame) ran an experimental continuous still here under special licence and, in its heyday, Kirkliston occupied a 12-acre site, required six Excise Officers and a Supervisor, and fed between 400–500 prizewinning pigs with the by-products and waste from six substantial pot stills* and a Coffey still capable of distilling 3,500 gallons of wash per hour.

Yet this huge and important operation, established in 1795, was abruptly closed in 1920 following a fire some years previously. It never worked as a distillery again. Today, most of the site has been cleared.

But rumour tells that a few bottles survive – treasured artefacts in private collections. It's highly improbable that any more will surface (if they did, they would be scrutinized very carefully indeed) and the existing relicts are unlikely to come to auction. No one will ever drink Kirkliston whisky again.

My name is Ozymandias, king of kings:
Look on my works, ye Mighty, and despair!'
Nothing beside remains. Round the decay
Of that colossal wreck, boundless and bare
The lone and level sands stretch far away§.

Shelley's 'Ozymandias' is a meditation on the nature of fame and worldly glory. Just as 'two vast and trunkless legs of stone' and a 'shattered visage' were all that remained of proud Ozymandias' monument, so all that we have today of this once sprawling powerhouse are some random bottles and photographs of the site prior to its redevelopment.

Yes, sadly, that's it. The End. It's finished: the Ozymandias of whisky.

* Interestingly, the condensers of all six were linked and fed a single worm tub 'of a most primitive pattern.'
§ From 'Ozymandias' by Percy Bysshe Shelly (1792–1822), published 1818.

53

Producer   William Grant & Sons Distillers Ltd
Distillery   Ladyburn, Girvan, Ayrshire
Visitor Centre   No
Availability   Very rare

Ladyburn

The enigmatic and quite private William Grant & Sons (they own Glenfiddich and The Balvenie, remember) have a splendid single malt distillery tucked away down in a quiet corner of Ayrshire, near Girvan. It's called Ailsa Bay, after the large volcanic plug you can see just offshore in the Clyde, Ailsa Craig*. So far it hasn't been released as a single malt, as all of it is required for Grant's blended whiskies. But we live in hope.

But that's not the first time single malt whisky was made here. Ailsa Bay, originally known as Girvan, was built as a grain distillery in 1963 to ensure supplies of single grain for blending, after Grant's had a disagreement with the Distillers Company Limited over how whisky was marketed. It's suggested that, in consequence, supplies of DCL's grain whiskies were to be restricted, hampering Grant's development. So, wishing to be as self-reliant as possible, they installed a small single malt plant here in 1966, consisting of two pairs of stills.

That single malt was known as Ladyburn, which is what we have here. Not really a separate distillery, as such, as it was contained in the giant Girvan complex§, it operated only until 1975 and was actually dismantled the following year. Some say the stills have subsequently been used to produce vodka for the Virgin brand but I have been unable to confirm that. Not that it actually matters. I wouldn't know what to do with a bottle of vodka.

Such a short life means that Ladyburn made one of the briefest appearances as a distillery in recent years, giving it a certain celebrity (or should that be notoriety) and an unwitting and entirely unintended place as a legendary whisky.

Independent bottlings crop up from time to time, generally labelled 'Ayrshire'. There have been several very limited official releases and rumour has it that a few casks remain to be bottled. No doubt these will be eked out at ever-higher prices to capitalise on this lost distillery's quixotic claim to fame.

I recall my one, rather limited, tasting as notably fruity with some spice development. It was a long time ago though… Then again, if you get hold of a bottle you're unlikely to drink it anyway.

You can find more on the fascinating story of Girvan and the man behind it earlier in this book.

* If, by any chance, you should require a 220-acre island complete with ruined castle, a small cottage, a lighthouse, a quarry and a gannet colony, it could be yours for £1.5m. Or make them an offer.
§ Hendrick's Gin is also made here. Bet you didn't know that.

Producer   Diageo
Distillery   Lagavulin, Islay
Visitor Centre   Yes
Availability   Widespread

www.malts.com

Lagavulin
Distiller's Edition

As early as 1930, Aeneas MacDonald in *Whisky** was describing Lagavulin as enjoying 'almost legendary fame'. He goes on: 'The other day I met a man who during his life as a recruit in the army was kept awake for hours in the night by the prolonged rhapsodies of two Highlanders, men who had nothing else in common in the world but their affection for and praise of Lagavulin.'

But even its devotees would admit that it's demanding stuff: one of the most forceful and full-flavoured of whiskies, even by Islay's demanding standards.

Back in the 1970s (and, for all I know, earlier) the official bottlings carried the date 1742. I recall that very well, because it's the same date as J A Devenish & Co. Ltd, the brewers, were founded. Early in my strange and varied career in the drinks industry, I was working in their Weymouth office when, as the token Scot, I was called to the Wines and Spirits Department to taste a bottle of Lagavulin returned by a pub on the grounds that it had 'gone off'. 'No,' I assured them, 'it's supposed to taste like this.' The Wines Director, wise in the ways of the world, looked quizzically over his spectacles at the preposterous stripling standing before him§ and slowly turned to his clerk. With due solemnity he pronounced the verdict. 'No product designed for human consumption could possibly taste like this. Refund the customer.'

So which Lagavulin did I choose? Some favour the older bottles that may still be found, especially those carrying the White Horse branding; some the annual Diageo Special Releases; and some the 12 Year Old expressions from the late 1970s, bottled for markets like The Netherlands. But at that point we are getting just a little recherché – into anorak territory, you might say. So, on the grounds of both accessibility and for the fact that it revealed new and unexpected facets of Lagavulin's character, I nominate the first ever Distiller's Edition. Distilled in 1979 and released in 1997, this was finished in Pedro Ximenez casks to add even more richness and sweetness. Other sherry casks followed, to general delight.

This might be expensive now (well, it is actually) but you do get a full litre. Just don't blame me if it keeps you awake at night.

* Check out the entry for his Dionysos Bromios Blend.
§ That would be me.

55

Producer
Distillery
Visitor Centre
Availability

Howgate Wine Co.
Bowmore, Islay
Yes
Auctions

Single Malt
From Casks Nº 2655/6/7
1967
LARGIEMEANOCH
SCOTCH WHISKY
12 YEARS OLD

Specially distilled in Islay
and bottled in Scotland
for The Howgate Wine Co. Ltd.
Cumberland Street Edinburgh.

95° PROOF   54·2% VOL.
26²⁄₃ FLOZ.   75.7cl.

Largiemeanoch

It may be a trifle simplistic but the world of whisky probably divides into those who have heard of Largiemeanoch and everybody else. There is an even more exclusive group who have actually tasted it.

We are dealing with something pretty arcane here and that inevitably adds to its allure. In fact, it's simply Bowmore by another name. Largiemeanoch was the name given to a very small number of private bottlings produced in the late 1970s for the Howgate Wine Co. of Cumberland Street, Edinburgh. Later the same name was used for whisky bottled for The Whisky Connoisseur, a firm in Biggar in Lanarkshire who marketed themed collections of miniatures to the collectors' market. Though still quite desirable, these are nothing like as highly regarded today as the Howgate Wine Co. expressions.

So far as I can ascertain, there were only two of these – the 12 Years Old shown here and a 10 Years Old. It's just a guess but I suggest that the latter was the first to be released. It was the outturn of just one cask and so there would have been fewer bottles than the 12 Years Old, which was a vatting of three casks – my hypothesis is that the first sold so well that Howgate Wine Co. needed more for their customers.

The 12 Years Old was bottled at cask strength (54.2%) in a simple flask-shaped bottle with a plain label with hand-written text. Occasionally a bottle will turn up at auction and you might expect to have to pay four figures to make it yours.

Bowmore from this period is keenly sought after and, like the bottling by the Italian independent Samaroli (see separate entry, as this itself is a whisky spoken of in hushed terms), this may be regarded as coming from an outstandingly productive period for the distillery when it was still in private, Scottish, family ownership.

Again, like the Samaroli Bouquet Bowmore, this was very highly rated by the Malt Maniacs group on the Whiskyfun website (if you haven't checked this out yet, you should – but leave yourself plenty of time, for this is whisky porn of the highest class). Their tasting note is lyrical and generous in its praise. It does, however, raise the interesting question of how far extended aging in the bottle contributes to eventual quality. You'll hear it said that whisky doesn't change once it's bottled (assuming you don't open it). I'm not so sure, believing that it almost certainly does change but, due to its strength, it does so very, very slowly. But if old bottles do evolve in flavour; the problem then becomes that there are no reference samples to check them against.

As I say, you've either tasted this or you haven't. I'd love to tell you how fabulous it is but I'd be making it up. I had heard of it as a whisky of fabled quality, though, so at least I knew what it was.

56

Producer
Distillery
Visitor Centre
Availability

Diageo
Mannochmore, Elgin, Morayshire
No
Auctions and specialists

www.loch-dhu.com (merchant site, not official distillery site)

Loch Dhu

Mannochmore is a perfectly inoffensive Speyside distillery operated by Diageo, with its output almost entirely devoted to whisky for blending.

However, between 1996 and 1997 it was home to the short-lived experiment that brought the world Loch Dhu ('the Black Loch' in Gaelic). In case you were in any doubt about the contents of the bottle, the label spelled it out – this is 'Black Whisky'.

According to many critics (and there are a few) this is a leading contender for the title of 'Worst Whisky in the World'. I'm not entirely sure that's fair. Firstly, it's an entirely subjective judgement and Loch Dhu has its fervent devotees. Secondly, I've tasted some utterly vile 'whiskies' from some of the new wave of craft distilleries that I would hesitate to use to scour the sink and Loch Dhu isn't that bad. I'm feeling in a benevolent mood, so no names. Also the one I particularly recall has improved greatly since that first memorably revolting taste.

It is very black, however. According to the distillers, this was due to the skilled use of 'double-charred' casks. Much the same effect could doubtless be achieved by adding thumping great dollops of spirit caramel, routinely used in some blended whiskies (and a few single malts) to standardise the colour. Though perfectly legal, it is something that whisky enthusiasts deplore.

Such was the opprobrium heaped on the head of Loch Dhu that it was pretty quickly withdrawn. (Officially due to portfolio rationalisation, following the creation of Diageo). Even at a modest £10 a bottle when launched it was vilified. Again, that seems in retrospect a trifle harsh: we can't criticise the whisky industry for lacking innovation and then comprehensively trash their products when they try. We have to be grown up about this and accept that not every experiment will work.

But here's the irony. Such is Loch Dhu's notoriety that it has now become a collector's item, with bottles fetching up to £200 – more for the 1 litre pack with gift box. There is even a specialist website devoted to selling the few remaining bottles (see opposite) and a 'tribute whisky' (if there is such a thing) known as Cu Dhub.

57

Producer
Distillery
Visitor Centre
Availability

Living

Chivas Brothers Ltd
Longmorn, Morayshire
No
Limited

www.longmornbrothers.com

Longmorn

Founded in 1893 during the great whisky boom immediately prior to the spectacular Pattison crash*, at a time when fortunes were made and lost and many of today's best-loved distilleries were built[§], Longmorn has long been highly regarded as a blending whisky. That keeps it busy, but also keeps it anonymous.

Lots and lots of its spirit goes into excellent blends such as Chivas Regal and Royal Salute but it's hardly ever seen as a single malt. There was a very nice 15 Year Old version available a few years ago but that was withdrawn in 2007 and replaced with a rather more snappily dressed 16 Year Old expression. Not everyone was happy.

I took it as good news at the time, thinking that Chivas Brothers were about to get serious (at last) about Longmorn as a single malt. I began to dream of other, older expressions (they did once release a 25 Years Old to commemorate the distillery's centenary, but only for staff and guests) and the deliciously tantalising prospect of a visitor centre, but it was not to be.

The marketing juggernaut rolled on; the latest whisky boom meant that more and more whisky was required for luxury blends and the moment passed. Encouragingly, though, Longmorn has just been expanded so we can hope for some good news in the future.

For, make no mistake about it, this is quality stuff. For its complexity, the elegant balance of weight and subtle smoothness, and for the huge nose and extended finish, this enjoys legendary status among blenders – and now you know about it as well.

It really is a classic, underrated and sadly nothing like as widely available as you might have hoped. There aren't even very many third party bottlings out there, so tightly is the stock coveted by the blending industry.

And that really says it all.

'A crack Highland malt,' a blender might observe (well, an old-fashioned one who speaks like a character from a P. G. Wodehouse story). That means it's ripping, top-hole stuff, don't you know.

* Keep reading; you will learn more about them shortly.
§ How comes it to be, you might not unreasonably ask, that so many distilleries date from the late 19th century, if whisky is so ancient? The industry would really rather you didn't ask, thank you very much.

58

Producer
Distillery

Visitor Centre

Availability

Lost

Chas. Mackinlay & Co
The blending records have been lost
so no one knows
Canterbury Museum, New Zealand,
or Cape Royds, Ross Island,
Antarctica (special permission and
woolly jumpers required)
Buried in the ice

http://whiskythaw.canterburymuseum.com | www.theshackletonwhisky.com

Mackinlay's
Rare Old Highland Malt

In 1907 British explorer Ernest Shackleton set off in his ship *Endurance* to lead the British Antarctic Expedition. Base camp was established at Cape Royds on Ross Island. Today this site has been preserved exactly as the expedition left it, as part of an Antarctic Specially Protected Area, governed by a management plan which aims to conserve and interpret one of the principal areas of early human activity in Antarctica.

So far so good. What interests us is that these boys clearly had a serious interest in keeping out the cold – and didn't just rely on their thermal undies. To which end, they contacted the Glen Mhor Distillery in Inverness, Scotland to order 46 cases of Mackinlay's Rare Old Highland Malt. We don't know how much the chaps drank on the way there but when they got to Antarctica they popped a few crates under their hut for safe keeping. Incidentally, when you think about the fact that they had to haul everything by hand (OK, with a few doggies to help), they clearly attached considerable importance to their evening dram.

Anyway, fast forward 102 years and a team from Canterbury Museum, New Zealand, succeeded in chipping one crate out of the ice, presumably very carefully, and taking it back to the museum to be thawed out. A specially built cool room was constructed and the whisky was slowly warmed up, enabling the team to examine the contents and eventually lift out several intact bottles labelled 'Mackinlay's Rare Old Highland Malt Whisky'.

Eleven bottles of the 114-year-old whisky have been recovered, of which remarkably ten appear perfectly intact, despite their labels having deteriorated. The wording 'British Antarctic Expedition 1907 Ship Endurance' is still visible on some of the bottles.

Whyte & Mackay's Master Blender Richard Paterson persuaded Canterbury Museum to extract a sample of the whisky which he was able to replicate and which is now sold under the name Mackinlay's – Shackleton The Journey. So now you can taste something resembling the whisky our great-great-grandfathers might have drunk. Those fortunate few who have tasted both say that the replica bears a remarkable resemblance to the original.

Just as well there's a replica, at an affordable £99 or so, as the museum plan to return all 11 bottles to their frozen tomb without touching a drop. What a waste!

Too much ice for my taste.

59

Producer
Distillery

Visitor Centre
Availability

Mackie & Co
Malt Mill – now 'absorbed' into
Lagavulin, Islay
Yes – Lagavulin
On show at Lagavulin Distillery
Visitor Centre

Malt Mill

They called Lord Byron 'mad, bad and dangerous to know', while 'Restless' Peter Mackie was famously described by the prodigiously talented Sir Robert Bruce Lockhart* as 'one third genius, one third megalomaniac and one third eccentric' – Mackie was not a man to be crossed.

In 1907 he held the sales agency for Laphroaig, the smoky Islay single malt, but this was withdrawn, for reasons now obscure. After a legal battle, which he lost, he simply decided to build his own distillery to provide himself with a similar style of whisky and, thus, the following year Malt Mill was born.

The tiny plant lay within the walls of Lagavulin and there Mackie determined he would produce a whisky to rival Laphroaig. It never did, despite him hiring staff from his old adversary. Presumably the make found its way into his most famous creation, White Horse, noted to this day for its subtly peaty taste and it certainly featured in his Mackie's Ancient Scotch brand.

But Malt Mill's fame today rests on its appearance on film – firstly (and rather more authentically) in a charming STV documentary about Islay, the imaginatively titled *Whisky Island* (1963 – you can view a clip on the Scotland on Screen website) and, secondly and more recently, in Ken Loach's award-winning movie, *The Angels' Share*, where the protagonists contrive to steal some whisky from a fantastically valuable 'lost' cask of Malt Mill.

Ironically, just as casks of real Malt Mill appeared on Scotland's TV screens in that first documentary production, the distillery had closed and been absorbed into Lagavulin where it has evolved to become a reception centre. There you can see the curious little bottle illustrated – a precious sample of the very last make, dated June 1962. Today it's treated with all the reverence due to a holy relic and handled only with gloves. By the look of the wax seal and the crudely handwritten label, no one was quite so impressed back then.

Sadly, unlike the story told in *The Angel's Share*, there is no lost cask of Malt Mill. If there were, no doubt it would fetch the fantastic price suggested in the film. So the little bottle of new make Malt Mill survives as evidence of a legendary whisky and a strange, driven man.

I didn't really care for *The Angel's Share*[§], thinking it lazy, cynical and dystopian with a cliched and stereotypical view of Glasgow and Scotland, but it did help bring a legendary whisky to the attention of a wider audience and the kilt gag is quite funny.

But it's nothing like Laphroaig, it would appear. Perhaps the angels could tell us.

* Journalist, author, secret agent, British diplomat and footballer. He also wrote a book about whisky: something of a show-off then.
§ Apart from Charlie MacLean's bit, of course. He gives a very convincing impression of himself.

60

Producer
Distillery
Visitor Centre
Availability

www.popcornsuttonswhiskey.com

Marvin 'Popcorn' Sutton

Marvin 'Popcorn' Sutton may not have been, as he liked to claim, the last of the moonshiners but he was certainly the most effective at perpetuating the myths of the Tennessee hillbilly distiller. He dressed the part, grew the wild and bushy beard you might have imagined and cheerfully hammed up the role for the TV cameras that came to follow him into the hills.

Born in 1946 into a long-line of bootleggers, with Scots-Irish roots, Sutton largely avoided the law, despite his fondness for publicity (he wrote a book on moonshining, released a video and featured in documentaries and films). Perhaps inevitably, the law won and in 2008 he was sentenced to 18 months in jail, after having offered to sell a batch of whiskey to a Federal Agent.

However, Popcorn came to a sorry end when he committed suicide in his beloved Ford Fairlane*, seemingly to avoid that prison term. He belongs here as much for the part he played in bridging the gap between a long tradition of moonshine distillers and today's micro-distillers, as for his own personal legend, polished as it undoubtedly was by his innate marketing skills.

This being America there is naturally a profit to be made from his legacy. While his family wrangle over various rights, his apprentice Jamey Grosser has the recipe for Popcorn's 'shine and he showed him his techniques. A legal distillery has now been opened to produce Popcorn Sutton's Tennessee White Whiskey[§]. Country singer Hank Williams Junior is a co-owner. (There had to be a country singer in there, really. In fact, I'm surprised they don't have a NASCAR driver as well. Just you wait.)

They had hardly moved on from Mason jars and started marketing this seriously before Jack Daniels' Properties (part of the mighty Brown-Forman Corporation) raised a legal action against them for passing off, claiming that the bottle shape and label will 'deceive and confuse the public'. JD, of course, are now marketing their own unaged spirit (a rye) to cash in on the craze for white whiskey – though one could hardly confuse their behemoth of a distillery in Lynchburg with the tiny Popcorn distillery in Nashville.

Before the Scots in the back of the class start sniggering at all this, just remember that George Smith of The Glenlivet was an illicit distiller before he came over all respectable, and even then he carried a loaded pistol when about his business, and that was less than 200 years ago.

It's the last damn run of likker I'll ever drink. I'm sticking to the aged stuff.

* His 'three jug car' – so called because he swapped three jars of 'likker' for it.
[§] In other words, moonshine or new make. 'White Whiskey' is the polite new name the marketing guys came up with to describe the legitimate sale of new make from a licensed distillery. Moonshine is the bootleg, illegal stuff.

61

Producer
Distillery
Visitor Centre
Availability

The
MICHAEL JACKSON
Special Blend

Michael Jackson was perhaps the most
admired whisky writer and taster the
world has seen. He travelled relentlessly,
seeking out whiskies from far-flung
places and brought their flavours to life
with unrivalled eloquence. This currently
limited world whisky produced in his
honour has been blended from Michael's
private collection containing whiskies
from many countries and adjusted for
balance to produce a very fine dram that
we hope he would be proud to drink

LIMITED EDITION
1 OF 1,000 BOTTLES
BOTTLED *2009* FEBRUARY

BOTTLED IN SCOTLAND BY
WHISKY MAGAZINE AND BERRY BROS. & RUDD LTD. LONDON SW1

Michael Jackson Blend

In Memoriam: Michael Jackson (27th March 1942 – 30th August 2007)

To those of us who knew Michael – and I first met him in Czechoslovakia in February 1984 – it still seems strange and uncomfortable that he's not around. Though his death was a shock, it was hardly a surprise as he had been unwell for some years, suffering cruelly from Parkinson's Disease.

It does not help that he shared the name of a famous singer; I have on several occasions had to disabuse whisky neophytes of the curious notion that the owner of Bubbles the chimpanzee was an authority on whisky.

He was clearly not the first person to write about either beer or whisky, and arguably he was not the finest of stylists, being more a journalist than a writer (not a distinction that is widely appreciated but, in my opinion, a crucial one), but he was indisputably the most influential. For that he will long be remembered.

The many writers, journalists and bloggers who today comment on whisky all live in his shadow, whether or not they are even aware of it. It is an ironic commentary on the popularity that he did so much to create, that many in this new generation of whisky enthusiasts appear oblivious to the debt they owe.

Michael was also never in any haste to commercialise his reputation; indeed, he was quite other-worldly (especially for a Yorkshireman with a Jewish heritage) in matters financial. What mattered more to him was commenting on and sharing the drinks and the industry that he loved – he was a particular fan of the sherried styles of The Macallan, a passionate advocate for Islay whisky when it was in the doldrums, and early to recognise the special quality of Springbank.

On his death, *Whisky Magazine* gathered the extensive library of samples from his huge collection and, with the assistance of Doug McIvor of Berry Bros. & Rudd, vatted the opened bottles to create the base for this Michael Jackson Blend. A total of 1,000 bottles were created and sold to raise funds for the Parkinson's Disease Society.

It was a splendid and appropriate gesture and demonstrates the very high regard in which he was held. If you do not know his work, try to get a bottle of this. Then settle down with one of his books – preferably the originals, not the follow-ons where his name is exploited as a brand – and salute a true whisky legend.

Drink it. I believe it's what he would have wanted.

Producer	Chatham Imports
Distillery	Kentucky Bourbon Distillers, Bardstown, Kentucky, USA
Visitor Centre	No
Availability	Primarily USA

Michter's

The whiskey George Washington gave his Army

You don't hear too much about Michter's, especially outside of the USA, but it's a real piece of history. The whiskey originally distilled here was so valued that when the American War of Independence broke out, General George Washington purchased it for his troops as they suffered and died in their pitifully inadequate log cabins through the long, brutal winter at Valley Forge (1777–78).

Conditions were so severe that at least 2,500 soldiers died from cold and malnutrition. Washington wrote that 'unless some great and capital change suddenly takes place... this Army must inevitably... starve, dissolve, or disperse, in order to obtain subsistence in the best manner they can.'

Michter's, as the saying goes, was 'the whiskey that warmed the American Revolution.' Washington, of course, went on to become a distiller in his own right at Mount Vernon, not the least of his achievements. His contribution to the history of whiskey in the US shouldn't be underestimated so I've given Mount Vernon its own entry.

But distilling at Michter's goes back before Washington knew about it. In 1753, John and Michael Shenk, Swiss Mennonite farmers, began distilling rye here, making it, at the time of its closure, America's oldest distillery. Later it was known as Bomberger's and eventually Michter's.

Sadly the distillery is no longer operating. The Michter's name is a long-established and highly respected one but the vicissitudes in the fortunes of American whiskey meant that the distillery closed after a chequered history in 1989. Naturally, it's a National Historic Landmark but that's hardly the same as an operating plant. The condition of the buildings is generally poor and deteriorating and they have been described as an 'eyesore'.

New owners acquired the site in June 2011 and were quoted as saying: 'Our number-one priority is to clean it up and get it safe.' After which they plan to use it for warehousing and grain storage. It would be the ideal location for a craft distillery, however, so let us hope that they are sufficiently inspired by its heritage to give over at least a tiny corner to some new stills.

Meanwhile, a modest amount of whiskey is produced under the Michter's label for the current brand owners with a line-up including single barrel ryes, very small batch bourbons, single barrel bourbon, and unblended American whiskey.

The picture is Michter's Celebration Sour Mash, a limited edition bottling of aged casks. Fewer than 300 bottles were produced and they sold out in hours. Did I get any? What do you think?

Living

Producer	Diageo
Distillery	Mortlach, Dufftown, Morayshire
Visitor Centre	No
Availability	Suddenly and unexpectedly widespread

SPEYSIDE
SINGLE MALT
SCOTCH WHISKY

MORTLACH

was the first of seven
distilleries in *Dufftown*. In the
C19th farm animals kept in
adjoining byres were fed on
barley left over from processing.
Today *water* from springs in
the *CONVAL HILLS* is used to
produce this delightful
smooth, fruity single
MALT SCOTCH WHISKY

AGED 16 YEARS

Distilled & Bottled in SCOTLAND
MORTLACH DISTILLERY
Dufftown, Keith, Banffshire, Scotland

43% vol   70 cl

www.mortlach.com

Mortlach

Mortlach is one of the distilleries that, for many years, Diageo have kept to themselves. However, it does enjoy a stellar reputation among those in the know.

'Give us Mortlach,' the connoisseurs would cry, 'for it is meat and drink to us.' But steely hearted Diageo would not – could not – relent and spurned the piteous solicitations. Because all the Mortlach, bar a tiny quantity, was forfeit to the mysterious blenders, heirs to the secret recipes of Alexander Walker. From their high and forbidding eyrie, crouched over their tiny ledgers, they saw that it was good and determined that it should be rightfully theirs.

But now, even as this little book blooms on shelves both solid and virtual, comes news from their fortress that the prayers of the righteous are to be granted and Diageo will bring forth four –count them and wonder! – 'new' Mortlachs. The price has, of course, greatly increased.

Renowned for the Byzantine complexity of its distilling regime, which defies all explanation and, like the peace of God, passeth all understanding, Mortlach stands alone in Scotch whisky, unique in its strange and complex flavours. 'Meaty' (the standard descriptor) does it scant justice.

For years it was seen only in Diageo's original Flora & Fauna series, a mighty 16 Years Old whisky reeking of sherry and not for nothing known as 'the Beast of Speyside'. (There may have been some independent bottlings, but they were furtive, almost clandestine creatures of whisky's demi-monde and glimpsed only rarely.)

Now, in a move both dramatic and simple*, the distillery has been expanded by the straightforward expedient of building another one, identical in make-up, rising today where some old warehouses stood. The legendary 2.81 times distillation has been slavishly copied, as have the deliciously old-fashioned worm tubs. The result, everyone fervently hopes, will be to double production without changing 'this unique Scottish laboratory of flavour and drinking delight'§.

But it will be some years before anyone knows for sure that the spirit running from the new stills is indistinguishable from the original. Meanwhile, you may feast on these 'new' Mortlachs, confident that they are in fact old Mortlach. Alongside two further styles, which in the coy fashion of our age do not declare theirs, there are 18 and 25 Years expressions.

But perhaps they have been on a diet, for these whiskies are not, I feel, as 'meaty' as once their predecessors were. More corned beef than a hearty roast.

* Simple it may be. It also requires a lot of money.
§ So taken was I by this high-flown rhetoric from the normally sober-sided Diageo, that I have reproduced it here verbatim. Isn't it an exquisitely crafted example of purple prose?

64

Producer	Catfirth Ltd (but they don't actually make the whisky)
Distillery	n/a – this is a blend
Visitor Centre	No
Availability	Specialists

Muckle Flugga

'OVER WINTERED'
IN SHETLAND

Blended Malt Scotch Whisky

PRODUCT OF SCOTLAND

INDIVIDUALLY
SELECTED MALTS
FROM MAINLAND
SCOTLAND

LIMITED EDITION

40% vol   70cl   1442

Muckle Flugga

I was fully expecting to have an almost indecent amount of fun with this entry – and then this whisky, which I had believed to be a phantom, a thing of myth, a transient and ghostly mirage, a product of an over-excited imagination – turned out to actually exist.

I'd better explain. About 10 years ago there was a plan – a half-baked, ill-conceived, badly executed and poorly managed plan, if you ask me – promoted by one Caroline Whitfield and a company called Blackwood Distillers to set up a distillery on Shetland. Like a number of other whisky writers, I was very critical of it.

It's not actually such a bad idea. But such was the massive hype and exaggerated publicity that, when the whole thing turned out to be largely dependent on launching vodka and gin, the disappointment was felt from Unst to Uzbekistan. Ms Whitfield was revealed as a better publicist than entrepreneur and when folk discovered the (perfectly tasty) gin not to be distilled in Shetland (as at first glance you might reasonably have imagined) but in the rather less than bucolic surroundings of Airdrie, a certain cynicism set in. Relentless investigative journalism by the *Shetland Times* raised more questions and the company's inability to raise funds led to its eventual failure.

Muckle Flugga was to be a blended malt, 'over-wintered' on Shetland – a variation on aging hitherto unknown to the Scotch whisky industry. Around 2,000 bottles did apparently make it to the island off Unst but were then mysteriously spirited away in a daring heist from a Hampshire warehouse. Heaven only knows what they were doing there. And then, just as I began writing this book, a few bottles emerged.

To learn more about this whole sorry story, search online. It's only fair to conclude that Blackwood's Gin and Nordic Vodka are still around, albeit under different ownership and well rated by people who know about such things. But plans for a distillery on Shetland remain legendary among connoisseurs of life's absurdities.

Happily, a rather more experienced team are now looking into the feasibility of a Shetland micro-distillery, so it could happen. It's about time this had a happy ending.

As for Muckle Flugga, it's tasty enough but really it's just an excuse for me to tell you this story.

65

Producer
Distillery
Visitor Centre
Availability

Nikka
Nishinomiya, Japan
No
Auctions

Single coffey malt
12
YEARS

Limited Edition
Bottle No.   /3027

700ml   ウイスキー   55%vol

Nikka

Coffey Malt

The legendary Aeneas Coffey – an Irishman – changed the world of distilling forever when he patented his design for a continuous still in 1830. His name is honoured here on this rare and unusual product from Japan. Rare because a mere 3,027 bottles were produced, of which fewer than 1,000 made it to Europe, initially via the French whisky specialist La Maison du Whisky. These sold out fairly fast because this is a most unusual whisky.

And that's for two reasons. First it was distilled at Nikka's Nishinomiya Distillery, which has since been closed and given over to brewery operations, though the continuous Coffey stills have been moved to Miyagikyo. But mainly because it is the stills that make this really unusual, for this is malt whisky distilled in a column still.

As the observant among you will have already noticed, you can't do this with Scotch whisky. At least, you can but you have to call the resultant product 'single grain', which in my view it isn't. Lomond Distillers tried to market a version made in Scotland in their copper columns using a 100% malted barley malt, but fell foul of the Scotch Whisky Regulations. All their efforts to persuade the SWA to permit a special category were rebuffed; unfairly, some felt. Call me cynical, but it occurs to me that perhaps they would have got on better if they had been members…

Anyway, back to Japan, where this hails from. I'm personally quite excited by this type of innovation and experimentation. Why not, so long as the label makes it clear what you are buying?

Subsequently, a number of variants have been offered – single-cask expressions and also a single grain. Despite some rave reviews (and a few less-than-enthusiastic commentaries) this hasn't really caught on. Personally, I feel that's rather a shame (although producers of Scotch single malt are presumably quite happy).

But I don't think this is the end of the story. A column still allows you to make the raw material of whisky faster, cheaper and with greater consistency. Sooner or later some distillery somewhere, not constrained by Scotland's tight regulations, is going to successfully market a tasty product using this technology and some good-quality wood – and then the world of distilling will be turned upside down.

Just as it was by Aeneas Coffey close to 200 years ago. Rapid adoption of his innovation enabled the Scotch whisky industry to overtake its Irish rival. Could history repeat itself?

66

Producer
Distillery
Visitor Centre

Availability

Lost

J & J McConnell Ltd
Stromness, Orkney
No – but a charming museum
is nearby
Auctions

Old Orkney

Isn't this quite the loveliest whisky advertisement you have ever seen? It featured on postcards and, I think, showcards from 1900 to 1920 to promote the 'Old Orkney' brand of 'Real Liqueur Whisky' from the Stromness distillery which, as you will have guessed, is on Orkney.

It was visited by our old friend Alfred Barnard, who was quite taken with the place, especially the stills; he described one as 'the quaintest we have seen in our travels… its body is shaped like a pumpkin, and is surmounted by a similarly shaped chamber one fourth the size'.

There were at that time three (legal) distilleries on Orkney, all on the mainland (as Orcadians refer to their principal island) – Stromness, Scapa and Highland Park. The latter two have survived – though it was touch and go for Scapa for a while – and are prospering. Not so Stromness, which closed in 1928 and was demolished during WW2.

Very, very occasionally bottles of the original Old Orkney brand appear at auction. However, be aware that the name was briefly revived as a brand by Gordon & MacPhail. Those are not the bottles you are looking for, so go about your business. The last original bottle that I can trace sold in April 2012 for a fairly modest £2,500 (plus commission). That doesn't seem much for a real piece of Scotland's whisky history. Copies of the postcard (£20–£30 seems normal) and the odd water jug appear slightly more frequently on internet auction sites, from where they are pretty rapidly snapped up by collectors.

Bottles will be extraordinarily rare. Apart from the sheer implausibility of their survival for this length of time, the distillery was tiny and production very limited. So this really is a museum piece. Ironically, adjacent to where the distillery once stood is a small and rather charming museum staffed mainly by enthusiastic volunteers who will happily chat to you about the town's long and fascinating history and point out the small display case featuring material from the distillery.

The site itself is now occupied by some council houses, one of which was home for 28 years to George Mackay Brown, the celebrated writer and poet. Evidently there's more profit in whisky than poetry, or perhaps Brown felt less for money than he clearly did for the cratur. He once wrote of whisky*: 'What is it but the earth's rich essence, a symbol of all fruit and corn and cheerfulness and kindling?'

And isn't that an advertisement for whisky every bit as lovely as the Old Orkney postcard?

* The Orcadian, 11th January 1979.

67

Producer	Andrew Usher & Co.
Distillery	n/a – this is a blend, based on The Glenlivet
Visitor Centre	Yes – at The Glenlivet
Availability	Auctions

Old Vatted Glenlivet

This is a whisky that changed the world. Well, the world of whisky anyway.

To understand why, we first need to distinguish between 'vatting', which today describes the mixing of different whiskies from the same distillery, and 'blending' where more than one distillery's product is used. Historically, however, the terms were interchangeable and what we are looking at here is, arguably, the first recognised blend in the modern sense.

There were two Andrew Ushers in this Edinburgh-based family firm, generally recognised as the pioneers of blending. The original Andrew Usher (1782–1855) was a spirit merchant and agent for Smiths of The Glenlivet. He is thought to have experimented with vatting whisky in the 1840s but it was not until 1853 when, due to changes in legislation, it was possible to vat under bond that Old Vatted Glenlivet was launched. The firm grew rapidly and, with a further change in the law in 1860, blending as we would recognise it today took off.

Andrew Usher II entered the business as a Partner in the late 1840s. Given that his father was 71 by the date this product was launched, it is probable that most of the credit should fall to the younger man. Later, his successor Sir Robert Usher was to claim to the Royal Commission on Whiskey* that this transformed their export business to England, noting that after 1860 'the trade in Scotch Whisky increased by leaps and bounds'. Blended whisky had arrived and nothing would ever be the same again in the world of whisky.

By the end of the century, Andrew Usher had over 15,000 casks of whisky in his Edinburgh warehouse, was a founding shareholder and first Chairman of the North British Distillery, exporting successfully to Japan and able to donate £100,000 to the city of Edinburgh to build a concert hall (the Usher Hall).

However, the company ceased trading in 1918 and was purchased by J & G Stewart, a subsidiary of The Distillers Company. They continued to market the Old Vatted Glenlivet blend until some time in the 1970s. For the most part, these are the bottles that turn up on auction sites: a 19th-century bottle would be highly prized. J & G Stewart was itself dissolved in October 1995, but Old Vatted Scotch limped on until 1998.

The Usher name continues to be found on whisky in the USA in the form of Usher's Green Stripe, a 'value' blend often found in larger pack sizes. Sic transit Gloria mundi – it seems a poor legacy for one of the building blocks of modern Scotch.

* Yes, that *is* how they spelt it.

68

Luxurious

Producer	The Sazerac Company for J P Van Winkle & Son
Distillery	Buffalo Trace, Franklin County, Kentucky, USA
Visitor Centre	Yes – but for the distillery, not the brand
Availability	Very limited annual release

23 Year Old

Pappy Van Winkle's

Family Reserve
Kentucky Straight Bourbon Whiskey
Bottle # 46
750 ml • Alc 47.8% Vol (95.6 proof)

Bottled by Old Rip Van Winkle Distillery • Frankfort, Ken

www.oldripvanwinkle.com

Pappy van Winkle
Family Reserve 23 Years Old

If there was such a thing as royalty in the world of whiskey, the Van Winkles would be in line for a coronation. This is the whiskey that even billionaires can't buy. Every year they release tiny quantities – tiny – and a long, long waiting list of fans is disappointed.

The Van Winkles – real people by the way – have a distilling heritage dating back to the late 1800s, when Julian P. 'Pappy' van Winkle was a travelling salesman for the W L Weller wholesale company. After a somewhat tangled history, even by the standards of the American whiskey industry, which was so distorted by the pernicious effects of Prohibition and its aftermath, the business continues in the hands of Julian van Winkle III. Their products (bourbon and rye) are made for them and aged at the superb Buffalo Trace Distillery.

If you already know about this, then there's not much I can tell you but appreciate that, on the back of the worldwide revival of interest in bourbon, their products are now seen as the crème de la crème. Their youngest bourbon is 10 years old and this nectar is 23 years old (seriously ancient for bourbon and the last from the legendary Stitzel-Weller Distillery, which we shall meet elsewhere in this book). Go back that far and no one foresaw the explosion of interest in a type of whiskey that was virtually moribund at the time.

So not very much was made – and there will never be enough made to meet today's demand. The company is cautiously run and managed. They like the fact that there are waiting lists for the waiting list in liquor stores around the world, and they are all too aware that what the whiskey gods have given with one hand they might, in time, take away with the other.

So, if you see a bottle, grab it. And give me a call. Because, according to Julian Preston van Winkle III: 'There's nobody else in our situation. I can't think of another product, period. Ferrari? Lamborghini? But if you have the means, you can get one of those. That's not necessarily true with us. We have people with literally billions of dollars who can't find a bottle. They could buy a private jet in cash. They'd have an easier time buying our company.'

69

Producer	Pattisons Ltd
Distillery	n/a – this is a blend
Visitor Centre	No
Availability	At auction

THE BOOMING OF THE CANNON

is nothing to the "booming" of Pattisons' Whisky. Steady unfaltering attention to the object aimed at hits the mark and wins the battle. Pattisons have aimed at hitting the public taste for a pure, sound, fully matured, delicately flavoured whisky, and they have succeeded. Pattisons' Whisky is the Scotch spirit in its perfection—wholesome, stimulating, and cream-like. Pattisons' Whisky has fought its way to the front and will remain there.

Sole Proprietors:

PATTISONS, Ltd., Highland Distillers, **BALLINDALLOCH, LEITH,** and **LONDON.**

Head Offices: CONSTITUTION STREET, LEITH.

Pattisons

The works of Sir Walter Scott were enormously popular in 19th-century Scotland. Not for nothing is he referred to as 'the man who invented a nation'. So, in all likelihood, Robert and Walter Pattison studied Scott's *Marmion* as schoolchildren and perhaps even learned its most famous couplet by rote:

Oh! what a tangled web we weave
When first we practice to deceive!

What a shame they didn't pay more attention: so much trouble could have been avoided. I feel sure that Scott, who had done so much for whisky, was turning in his grave at the Pattisons' skullduggery and deceit.

The story is well known: the brothers inherited a small but perfectly respectable blending business, rapidly expanded it, floated it on the Stock Market, taking advantage of the spectacular whisky boom of the 1890s, and began inflating profits by passing off cheaper Irish whiskey as quality single malt from Glenlivet. Before long they went sensationally bust.

It was the Enron of its day and an international sensation. Several other businesses, essentially sound but for the error of having traded with the Pattisons, were also dragged down. Robert and Walter, who had 'sold' the same casks of whisky several times over to different customers, were ruined and went to prison for fraud; the reputation of whisky in general, and blending in particular, took a very severe knock and it was many years before the trade really recovered.

I can't decide if they were naïve and over-ambitious, caught up in their own publicity, or if they cynically planned the whole thing. What's certain is that while their star was in the ascendant it rose rapidly and burnt brightly, but when it fell to earth it was extinguished in recrimination and ruin. Fun while it lasted, no doubt, but this became, in the pious words of their liquidator, 'the most discreditable chapter in the history of the whisky trade.'

And that, of course, makes it interesting. From time to time a bottle of their whisky appears at auction. The last one I can trace sold for £1,900 – which seems cheap for such a piece of history.

The motto *'animo non astutia'* (by which they appeared to mean 'by courage not craft') appeared on much of Pattisons' packaging. But to judge by their antics and eventual sticky end, it's a fair guess craftiness was their undoing!

70

Producer
Distillery
Visitor Centre
Availability

The Number One Drinks Company
Port Charlotte, Islay
No
Mythical

Port Charlotte

Port Charlotte? Will it rise again? Can it?

The Port Charlotte Distillery (or Lochindaal as it was alternately known), worked on the shores of Lochindaal on Islay from 1829 until its final closure 100 years later. That wasn't that unusual a fate and, like many others lost at that time, the distillery and most of the buildings were eventually dismantled. Its demise passed largely unnoticed and unlamented. It wasn't for another 60 years or so that people began to pay much attention to the rather forlorn site.

It's just along from Bruichladdich, however, who since re-starting production in 2001 had been using the old dunnage warehouses to age their whisky. In 2007 the quixotic Mark Reynier, then MD of the then-independent Bruichladdich, announced that it would reopen Port Charlotte.

Quite how he planned to do this was never revealed in any great detail and the announcement appeared to take some of his colleagues by surprise (not for the first time, if we may credit rumour). The rest of the whisky world were certainly nonplussed (those who noticed, that is – some people had started to treat Mark's pronouncements with a certain disdain by then).

It seemed like a nice idea, if a little romantic and idealistic. However, if the money to restore Annandale in the Scottish Borders (also lost about the same time) could be found (and it has been), then I suppose there's no financial reason why Port Charlotte couldn't pull off a phoenix-like renaissance, however improbable.

But do we really need another revived distillery? Especially – let's be honest – this not particularly distinguished one?

Perhaps, instead, we should concentrate on looking forward, creating whiskies for the 21st century, rather than harking back to some imagined, misty, golden age of roaring, peat-soaked drams knocked out by some horny-handed sons of toil (sorry, that should of course read 'passionately hand-crafted by iconic artisans').

Thus far, Bruichladdich have limited themselves to designating their peated style as Port Charlotte and, in fairness, it has done well. I even bought and bottled a cask of it myself – 'whisky writer pays for stuff' – now that is legendary!

But a bottle of the original Port Charlotte? Well, that would be quite something.

71

Producer	Diageo
Distillery	Port Ellen, Islay
Visitor Centre	No
Availability	At auction

Port Ellen

Being of a nostalgic turn of mind I've elected to have a picture of the distillery rather than one of the many, many bottles you can find – at a price – from this silent Islay giant.

The distillery seems to have started around 1833 and was closed in 1983, so it had a pretty good run. Let's not forget it wasn't closed by accident – there was little or no demand back then for heavily peated whisky, either from the blenders or the nascent single malt market. The distillery needed a lot of money spent on it and Islay looked pretty down and out.

Things change, of course, but at the time closing it was a rational and understandable decision. However, quite unexpectedly, Islay and its whisky became fashionable, more and more so. There was, of course, a quantity of Port Ellen remaining in cask when the distillery was closed, and this is where things get interesting.

My friends at The Whisky Exchange kindly worked out for me that they had handled over 400 different bottlings of Port Ellen in the last seven years; although they pointed out that this flood of new releases is partly accounted for by those independent bottlers still holding stock and realising that their carefully hoarded casks are getting over the hill and won't be improving any further.

So, eventually, peat freaks and smoke heads are going to have to face the fact that, whether from Diageo or third-party bottlers, *there is no more Port Ellen* (a delicious frisson of *Schadenfreude* passes through me as I write these words). Presumably, prices will continue to rise, as they have done quite dramatically in recent years, with Diageo's Special Releases leading the way.

Yes, the evil capitalists who run Diageo had the temerity to more than double the price of their 2012 release, presumably after observing the instant gains made by speculators on various internet auction sites. I shudder to think what's going to happen when stocks finally do run out, but you can't really blame Diageo. They've got shareholders to think about. Here's the official version:

'*Stocks of Brora and Port Ellen are inexorably diminishing. Each year's limited-edition bottling releases one more fragment of whisky history that is unique, and can't ever be replaced. On top of that, Port Ellen and Brora are not merely rare, old and in great demand – they are judged by most qualified commentators to be of outstanding quality, and this year's edition will be no exception.*'

As a result, I haven't tried it for years. Can't afford it.

Producer	Sir John Power & Son (Irish Distillers Ltd)
Distillery	John's Lane, Dublin, and, today, Midleton, Cork, Ireland
Visitor Centre	Yes
Availability	Auctions and specialists

Power's

John's Lane

As I am forever reminding people, Irish whiskey was once a world leader. It may be enjoying something of a revival today but there was a time when it was indisputably number one.

If you doubt this, open up your copy of Barnard. If you don't have a copy of Alfred Barnard's *The Whisky Distilleries of the United Kingdom* then get one immediately. You should be able to pick up a decent first edition for around £3,000. Or one of the many excellent facsimiles for less than £25 on eBay.

He allocates six pages to his visit to the John's Lane Distillery in Dublin – *six pages*. If you're not convinced, take a look at the frontispiece. The stout gentleman in the wig standing in the somewhat improbably bucolic setting is James Power. Now ask yourself, out of all the images Barnard could have picked, why did he choose this one?

Because at the time he was writing, John's Lane was arguably the finest, most efficient and best organised distillery in the world*.

What's left today? Just a few buildings, a chimney, a clock and three enormous pot stills, arranged as sculptures in the grounds of what is now Ireland's National College of Art and Design. They bear silent witness to the destruction of a great industry. Today, Power's Gold Label, one of the first Irish whiskies to be bottled and the brand which secured the firm's reputation, is made by Irish Distillers Ltd in Midleton. It's a lovely drop, but a poignant reminder of what might have been had history taken a different course.

The John's Lane distillery, in decline by then, was closed in 1974 and largely demolished. A cruel fate for one of the true legends of Irish whiskey – and a salutary reminder to the tumescent Scotch whisky industry, increasingly puffed up on its own undoubted success that all things must pass.

Bottles distilled at the original John's Lane distillery still appear at auction. The Midleton expressions – Gold Label and Power's John's Lane (a lovely pot still whiskey) seem a pretty fair substitute. The John's Lane in particular tends to the more delicate and spicy end of Irish whiskey.

So this is sort of a ghost of a legend, but one that we can all enjoy.

* Mind you, the partners did stand Barnard a 'substantial luncheon' to which he recounts he did 'ample justice' and they sent him away with a flask of old make. In my experience, few journalists have been known to refuse such blandishments (all in the interests of research, it should be understood).

73

Producer Gordon & MacPhail
Distillery Glen Grant, Rothes, Morayshire
Visitor Centre Yes
Availability Only 85 bottles

Luxurious

Queen Elizabeth II
Diamond Jubilee Glen Grant

The Elgin-based merchants, bottlers and, these days, distillers to boot, Gordon & MacPhail are in their own understated way something of a legend themselves. Relatively few family-owned firms survive in the Scotch whisky industry and, excepting the Grants of Glenfiddich fame, certainly not any really large ones. That alone makes Gordon & MacPhail remarkable. When you add their shop in Elgin (a cathedral of whisky; many a strong man has been led weeping from its shelves, bewildered by the choice shimmering before him, like some apparition of the apotheosis of whisky), their extraordinary stocks, their ranges of obscure single malts, and their competitive pricing, perhaps I should be listing them in their own right.

But of recent years they have been releasing some exceptionally old whisky. Starting in 2010 with a Mortlach fully 70 years old, they followed this in 2011 with a similarly venerable Glenlivet and, for the Diamond Jubilee of Queen Elizabeth II, they brought forth this 60 Years Old Glen Grant.

Two thoughts occurred to me on tasting it: firstly, Glen Grant is a singularly underrated whisky (except in Italy where it has long enjoyed a strong following) and, secondly, whisky isn't supposed to last this long. Given the long-standing industry view that whisky lasts 20 to 25 years at the most in cask – keeping whisky longer than that was eccentric at best and downright foolhardy at worst. It would surely become woody and over-aged – 'slimy' was a term I heard employed.

It is true to say that not all whisky ages well beyond, say, the 25-year mark. However, this one has done. Like the monarch it celebrates, it has slowed with age but gained in dignity and quiet authority. It is a whisky to respect. Last time I looked, a few specialist merchants still had this available on their lists.

By the standards of these things, the £8,000 they will ask of you is cheap but you can still obtain Glen Grant from the 1936 distillation, bottled at 50 years of age, from Gordon & MacPhail for a more modest £3,500 or so; or explore the extensive range of private bottlings from this strangely underrated Speysider.

When I say I tasted it, it was more of a mini taste, a mere teaspoon full, a stain on the bottom of the glass rather than a tasting sample: merely an ephemeral sensation of dignity and old leather. But Charlie MacLean, one of Scotland's top whisky writers and a very sound judge, was there and he declared it 'very fine' so that's the verdict.

74

Producer
Distillery
Visitor Centre
Availability

Lost

Diageo
Rosebank, Falkirk
No
Occasional specialists, auctions a
Diageo Special Releases

RARE MALTS
SELECTION

This bottled vintage has been specially selected from the most
rare single malt stocks of rare or now extinct distilleries
in finest fillings of some export and vintage whiskies for
expert full strength for the enjoyment of the true connoisseur

NATURAL
CASK STRENGTH
SINGLE MALT
SCOTCH WHISKY

AGED **20** YEARS

DISTILLED 1981

ROSEBANK
DISTILLERY
ESTABLISHED 1840
FALKIRK, STIRLINGSHIRE

62.3%vol 70cl e

PRODUCED AND BOTTLED
IN SCOTLAND

LIMITED EDITION
BOTTLE

Rosebank

When someone proposes spending serious money recreating a distillery that was closed in 1993 you have to believe something interesting is going on. Perhaps a legend is in the making (or re-making) because this is a distillery and a whisky that has been sorely missed. If I sounded sceptical about reopening Port Charlotte that's because I am. This, however, is different.

Rosebank is, or rather was, a markedly traditional distillery on the banks of the Forth and Clyde Canal in Falkirk in Central Scotland. It's not the bonniest place in Scotland and the image of faded industrial semi-dereliction associated with the distillery at the time of its closure was not one that the marketing fraternity would have looked to promote. The distillery's site was heavily constrained by neighbouring buildings and by the canal itself; the equipment needed an expensive refit to meet environmental regulations and Glenkinchie Distillery was considered more than capable of producing all the Lowland single malt that Diageo required for the foreseeable future. So Rosebank was closed.

Would they like to turn the clock back and reverse that decision? You bet! But, 20 years ago it seemed like the right one and no one expected the resurgence of interest in true triple-distilled Lowland single malt, then somewhat simplistically written off as 'light'.

With a raft of independent bottlings, the sadly missed Flora & Fauna and Rare Malts series, and Diageo's ever-more-expensive Special Releases, Rosebank has come into its own.

The original distillery will never reopen. However, such is the reputation of its whisky that there are plans to revive its spirit. Buoyed up by the present wave of interest in boutique distilleries, The Falkirk Distillery Company intend to open a new distillery nearby. Initially there were plans to use the Rosebank name, resulting in Diageo (who retain the trademark) quickly explaining why that could not and would not happen. These plans seem to have stalled somewhat, however, with the promoters' website still promising an opening by November 2011.

It would appear that they have been overtaken by Scottish Canals (British Waterways bought the original buildings from Diageo in 2002), who are now promoting a mixed use regeneration scheme for the overall site. In September 2013, prospective tenants Arran Brewery received a £500,000 grant from Historic Scotland for their plan for a brewery, micro-distillery and visitor centre on the site.

One can't but wonder what Diageo would have been able to do with £500,000 of government money back in 1993, but at least the legend (or part of it) lives on.

75

Luxurious

Producer | John Dewar & Sons Ltd
Distillery | Royal Brackla, Nairn
Visitor Centre | No
Availability | Auctions

www.dewars.com

Royal Brackla
60 Years Old

For a little-known distillery – most of the output goes into the Dewar's blends – Royal Brackla holds a singular distinction. Or perhaps that should be a double distinction, for this is the only distillery to hold two Royal Warrants from British monarchs.

The first, dating to the days of William IV, was awarded in 1833 (or possibly 1835, accounts vary) and was the first Royal Warrant ever awarded to a whisky. On her accession to the throne, the new Queen Victoria wasted no time and promptly renewed it on 15th November 1838 (a Thursday, as it happens, rather damp and overcast). She seemed keen on whisky (see next entry).

And that's been that ever since. Today our monarch prefers a Dubonnet and gin cocktail. There's no accounting for taste, I suppose; the whisky industry is holding its breath for the arrival of King Charles III, who is known to be partial to something peaty. Fat chance of Brackla's hat-trick there, then.

Time was this was a turbulent place. The original recipient of both those Warrants, Captain William Fraser, was regularly fined for breaches of the distilling regulations and the gauger (Excise Officer) Joseph Pacy wrote: 'I know that I never encountered a man either in or out of the service that tested my courage, my prudence, or my honesty, more than this same distiller.'

But the whisky has long been highly regarded. In 1828, the *Aberdeen Chronicle* described it as 'this much-admired spirit'; the two Royal Warrants remain unrivalled and Aeneas MacDonald praised it as 'one of the dozen or so best whiskies made in Scotland'.

A very limited commemorative bottling of a 35 Years Old was issued recently to mark Brackla's 200th anniversary (a year late and in a rather vulgar bottle, reminiscent of Chambord liqueur) but the legendary reputation rests on the Warrants and the rather more modestly packaged 60 Years Old from the late 1980s. Unbelievably, this venerable spirit was given away to guests at the distillery's reopening in 1991: I do hope that they appreciated it. Since then the distillery has been acquired by Bacardi.

I'm not alone in wishing that they would do more with the single malt. There have been a couple of very limited releases, but their heart really isn't in it. Here's what people used to think:

'THE KING'S OWN WHISKY, distilled expressly for the use of his Majesty at Fraser's Royal Brackla Distillery, Inverness, is perhaps the only malt spirit which proves alike congenial to the palate and constitution of connaisseurs [sic] of every country.' *Morning Post,* 7 May 1836

76

Producer
Distillery
Visitor Centre
Availability

Diageo
Royal Lochnagar, Deeside
Yes
Specialists

Royal Lochnagar
Selected Reserve

Imagine you've just opened a distillery. You've got plenty of competition and you need a marketing edge.

So what would you do? Simples. You drop a quick email to some young Royals – Kate and Wills, for example – and casually enquire if they wanted to pop round to see the distillery. 'Bring George,' you'd add. And, next day, there they would be. One quick tour later and, hey presto, you add 'Royal' to the name of your fledging operation. Brand identity problem solved; successful future assured.

Back in 1848 that's pretty much what the enterprising John Begg did at Lochnagar. It's about half a mile from Balmoral Castle*, which had just been leased by a young Queen Victoria and her beloved Prince Albert. Begg heard that the Queen, Prince Albert and their children were staying and, pretty confident that they would be tired of playing Scrabble, he invited them round. And, next day, round they came.

Liking everything they saw, they raised no objection to the distillery renaming itself Royal Lochnagar. Much snappier than New Lochnagar. Sales increased handsomely; trebles all round.

Today, this little distillery is one of only two that can carry the Royal title (Royal Brackla is the first, though we don't hear very much about it at present). The current operators, Diageo, maintain Lochnagar in apple-pie order with a cracking little visitor centre (busloads of tourists head for nearby Ballater and a chance to bump into the Queen picking up her groceries – for the most part, they're disappointed so they need a stiff drink) and some elegant corporate entertaining and training spaces.

Some of the make – and there isn't a lot, as this is one of the smaller distilleries in Scotland, with an annual output of less than 500,000 litres – goes into blends, particularly Johnnie Walker. The whiskies that went into the spectacular Johnnie Walker Diamond Jubilee decanters, which have an entry all to themselves, were married and bottled here and if you visit the distillery you can still see the empty casks on display. Face it; that's as close as you're going to get to a £100,000 whisky.

Today the Selected Reserve comes in a blue box and it remains a right royal whisky.

* They actually knocked the old castle down. The one you see today is Victoria and Albert's creation, which played a huge part in making Scotland fashionable in the 19th century. Royal patronage was everything, you see.

77

Producer

Distillery
Visitor Centre
Availability

Scottish Malt Distillers
(a subsidiary of DCL)
St Magdalene, Linlithgow, Ireland
No
Limited

AGED 30 YEARS

LINLITHGOW

NATURAL CASK STRENGTH SINGLE MALT WHISKY

DISTILLED YEAR 1973 · BOTTLED IN 2004

A regal Lowland malt, this complex natural cask-strength Linlithgow
makes an astounding aperitif. Fruity nose. Light body. Fresh fruit,
engaging medicinal development. Dries to a ghost of a finish.

PRODUCT OF SCOTLAND

St Magdalene

The original St Magdalene was, of course, Mary Magdalene, a hugely important figure in the New Testament and in Jesus's life, crucifixion and resurrection. She is considered a saint and revered for her courage and steadfastness.

A very special name, then, for any distillery to carry. Its site was an important one in historic Linlithgow, a small town in West Lothian which from the 12th century played a significant role in Scottish history. Sadly, it has been poorly served by successive generations of planners and much of the historic centre has been lost. Prior to the distillery, there was a lazar house* on the site, known as St Magdalene's Hospital. The distillery took its name from that, though it was also referred to and its whisky bottled as Linlithgow.

The distillery was established sometime between 1765 (possibly by Sebastian Henderson) and 1798, but moved to the St Magdalene site in 1834. In 1912 it was acquired by the Distillers Company who renovated it in 1927. Given the general state of the whisky industry at that time, this suggests that the distillery was important and well-regarded by them. It may also have been because, as a Lowland single malt, it was of particular importance in blending. However, neither this nor its historical significance was enough to save it from the 1983 wave of closures§ and the distillery has subsequently been converted into housing.

Its reputation has been rehabilitated in recent years, largely due to releases of the remaining stocks in Diageo's Rare Malts and Special Release series. Independent bottlings can also be found, though will presumably become rarer and rarer as stocks are exhausted.

Today, although not as highly regarded as Rosebank, its sister Lowlander, Linlithgow's closure is seen as a tragic and regrettable loss. It's hard to imagine that it could happen today. Even if the distillery needed substantial investment, its location near Edinburgh, long history and the fact that it is a Lowland whisky would ensure its survival. If only it could have hung on for another 20 years or so it would be with us still.

It seems probable that appreciation of this distillery, little heralded during its long lifetime, will grow in inverse proportion to the rarity of the surviving few casks. It is beginning to develop something of a small cult following, such that its name may outlive the last of its whisky.

* My editor says I should explain that this was a hospital for people suffering from leprosy. As I take you to be well-read and highly educated, I assumed you would know that.

§ Remember the 'whisky loch'? The closures were a result of massive over-production of the previous decade.

78

Producer
Distillery
Visitor Centre
Availability

Samaroli
Bowmore, Islay
Yes
Auctions

Luxurious

BOWMORE

75 cl.
53° GL

Bouquet 1966
Full Strength
Pure Islay Malt
Scotch Whisky
SAMAROLI

Samaroli Bowmore

Though originally bottled at relatively modest prices for the enjoyment of Italian connoisseurs, the original Samaroli bottlings from the 1980s have now attained legendary status – perhaps none more so than this cask strength (53% abv) Bowmore in the renowned 'Bouquet' series. With only 720 bottles produced and, presumably, many drunk at the time, this is now a real rarity but some remain in collections and if you are very, very lucky it's possible a bottle may turn up at auction.

But expect to pay handsomely for tasting this exceptional whisky. First, however, a word of explanation concerning Samaroli. The company was founded in 1968 by Silvano Samaroli, who began bottling single casks of carefully selected single malts, based on his own personal judgement, a deep love of Scotch whisky, and many visits to Scotland. At the time he was one of the very few to bottle single malt and arguably the first person outside the UK to do so.

Fortunately he was possessed of a discriminating palate and, at a time when the selection and bottling of a single cask would have been regarded as mildly eccentric at best by most of the industry, he was able to secure some remarkable whiskies. As a result, his reputation grew and his products (also including rum) became increasingly sought after.

This Bowmore is a relatively modest 18 years of age, having been distilled in 1966 and bottled in 1984. In fact, Samaroli is not an enthusiast for very old whiskies, having stated his belief that, 'Great malts can't mature in wood for more than 25 or 30 years. After this, they lose body and structure.'

There has been some criticism of Bowmore's distillation style during much of the 1980s but all thoughtful commentators agree that this dates from a golden age of quality for Bowmore. The exceptionally elegant and stylish label gives no information on the cask from which the whisky was drawn but it is quite light in colour, with delicate gold hints. Having been fortunate enough to try this whisky, I can confirm that it fully lives up to its stellar reputation.

Beloved of enthusiasts, I can do no better than to quote Malt Maniac Serge Valentin's commentary on the influential Whiskyfun website where he concludes by describing this as 'One of the very few total winners I've been lucky to be allowed to taste' and awarding it 97/100. Now, I'm not one for marking whiskies but M. Valentin has drunk a lot of very fine whisky; anything he scores above 90 I would want to try.

79

Producer
Distillery

Visitor Centre

Availability

Lost

Scotch Malt Whisky Society
Glenfarclas, Ballindalloch, Morayshire
(allegedly)
Society premises in Leith, Edinburgh,
London & hotel partners
Lost and gone forever

Scotch Malt Whisky Society

Bottle 1:1

You probably have to be as long in the tooth as I am, and with as keen a sense of the ironies of life, to remember when the Scotch Malt Whisky Society was the *enfant horrible* of the whisky industry and cordially disliked by most of it.

The Society was formed in 1983 by Philip (Pip) Hills, one of those larger-than-life Edinburgh eccentrics which that douce, self-satisfied city throws up from time to time and consents to tolerate patiently, thus demonstrating to itself how liberal, open-minded and generally progressive it is, all the while luxuriating in its own bourgeois complacency. Some great architecture though.

The SMWS, being now a creature of the corporate world, has largely written Pip out of its history – even the self-consciously funky little film on its website showing its beginnings somehow neglects to mention his name*. So sanitised is this version of events that even his infamous Lagonda has mysteriously transmogrified into a VW Beetle. However, stepping back three decades to the society's formation (and longer to its roots), the SMWS was once a truly radical and innovative creation, subversive (in the best sense), entirely concerned with challenging orthodoxy, upsetting the established order and generally embracing an iconoclastic view of the world of whisky.

In the main, this consisted of bottling the then largely unknown and almost entirely unheralded product known as single malt whisky for its members; direct from the cask and, shockingly as it then seemed, at cask strength and non-chill filtered. It is a measure of the society's achievements that younger readers will have been entirely mystified by the preceding sentence. Trust me then when I tell you that in 1991 my then-boss, the then-MD of Glenmorangie, insisted that my membership of the SMWS must lapse as being 'inconsistent with my responsibilities to the company'. Today, of course, Glenmorangie own the SMWS.

Strictly speaking, this isn't the very first bottle, as a syndicate of friends preceded the creation of a formal organisation – but it will have to serve.

Society bottling 1.1 has long since been consumed, with only the bottle shown surviving in their archives. It, and the organisation it spawned, are legendary beasts, nonetheless, and I am gratified to honour both them and Hills (thus demonstrating my own liberal, open-minded and progressive views).

* In fairness, his buccaneering approach to commerce did later come close to bankrupting the Society and he was – correctly as he now acknowledges – 'encouraged' to move on.

80

Luxurious

Producer	J & A Mitchell & Co. Ltd
Distillery	Springbank, Campbeltown, Argyll and Bute
Visitor Centre	Yes
Availability	Auctions and possibly specialists

www.springbankdistillers.com

Springbank
1919

Springbank is a very unusual distillery. Mark Reynier, then CEO at Bruichladdich, once memorably described them as 'a very odd bunch of people' and observed 'they are not like other businesses'.

Of course, he was right about the last bit. But they don't want to be like other businesses and rather pride themselves on going their own way. One might observe in passing that, while Springbank is still there vigorously independent and apparently prospering, Bruichladdich has been acquired by Remy Cointreau and Mark no longer sits in the boss's chair.

So, for the record, Springbank is the oldest, independent, family-owned distillery left in Scotland; it is the only distillery in Scotland to carry out the full production process on the one site*, with traditional floor malting, maturation and bottling all undertaken in Campbeltown, and it has quietly been doing innovative and unusual things long before the rest of the industry caught up.

What about bottling a 50-year-old whisky? They're all the rage now and quite a number of distilleries have one on their shelves. Springbank released theirs in 1970. 1970?! No one else had dreamt of doing something like that.

There were only 24 bottles produced of Springbank 1919. Springbank, being Springbank, simply put it into a standard tall round bottle with a simple label. No engraved decanter, no silver stopper, no hand-crafted oak cabinet, and no leather-bound book from some famous whisky writer[§].

Once upon a time it entered the *Guinness Book of Records* as the world's most expensive whisky, but the distillery still had stocks until March 2009, when they sold their last two bottles. So that's 50 years to mature the whisky and 39 years to sell two dozen bottles.

That is, it must be admitted, a *little* odd.

I don't know what else to tell you about this: it's a museum piece from the most traditional of all distilleries, revered in whisky-loving circles and immune from all corporate trends, management fashions and constantly changing marketing campaigns. Good for them. I wish there were a few more like them.

Problem is, we'll probably have to wait another 50 years to try the next one.

* Well, of any scale, certainly. Smaller operations, such as Kilchoman, increasingly aim for complete integration.
§ Not even me. Proving that they do make mistakes some of the time. Dreadful, ghastly mistakes.

81

Producer J & A Mitchell & Co. Ltd
Distillery Springbank, Campbeltown, Argyll and Bute

Visitor Centre Yes
Availability Any decent specialist

www.springbankdistillers.com

Springbank
21 Years Old

I doubt that any reasonably well-informed whisky lover would deny Springbank a place on this list. It may not be quite as fashionable as once it was and they may no longer sell you a single cask to bottle yourself but it will be forever a whisky legend for keeping the name and tradition of Campbeltown distilling alive when all seemed lost.

Back in 1987, the well-known whisky writer Michael Jackson was an enthusiastic advocate for the distillery but noted mournfully that 'this very traditional plant has not produced for some years.' Not so very long after that the growth of interest in single malt whisky led to the distillery's steady revival and it developed something of a cult following, helped by its very obscurity. Judging by the elaborate tattoos I've seen on some enthusiasts it does inspire its devotees in strange and wonderful ways.

But which Springbank to choose? There is a strong argument for suggesting the 24 Years Old Local Barley bottling from 1990. In fact, despite its limited availability, I couldn't ignore its almost mythic status, so you will find that in a separate entry. In the late 1970s Samaroli also bottled Springbank (naturally) but, like the Local Barley, anyone owning one of these bottles would rather part with their first-born child than give up these legendary liquids.

There are, in fact, many independent bottlings to be found. Springbank, unlike their family-owned counterpart Glenfarclas, have always seemed happy to sell casks to third party bottlers with an apparently cavalier disregard for their brand name. This only serves to confuse those of us with limited resources, as many of these expressions are perfectly sound.

However, I would stick with the distillery's own bottling and you will have to go a long way, and pass many bars, to find something to surpass the annual release of the 21 Years Old. Unfortunately there is never very much available and it sells very quickly, at a fairly stiff price, to those in the know. I like to imagine them as whisky's Gollum, consuming it furtively at night, making a horrible swallowing noise in their throat, and gloating over it while racked with guilt at their own terrible part in its consumption.

Springbank's great rival was Glen Scotia, whose owner Duncan MacCallum drowned himself in Campbeltown Loch in 1930. It's never tasted quite the same since. Springbank – at 18 or 21 years – is, however, quite simply lip-smackingly good.

82

Producer
Distillery

Visitor Centre
Availability

Luxurious

J & A Mitchell & Co. Ltd
Springbank, Campbeltown, Argyll
and Bute
Yes
Auctions and specialists

Springbank
West Highland Malt

There are three entries for Springbank in this book.

That's remarkable for any distillery. For a small distillery about as remote as it's possible to be anywhere on Scotland's mainland and which, by any commercial logic, should have closed down in the 1980s (if not the 1920s) it is extraordinary.

But all three of the whiskies mentioned, even including the 21 Years Old which you can get if you try hard enough, enjoy near-mythic status among whisky lovers. This is in part due to its adherence to a somewhat idiosyncratic method of production, in part due to its stubborn survival against the odds but mainly due to the outstanding quality of some whiskies produced in the 1960s which were bottled as the West Highland Malt series. Look for the original dumpy bottles; there is a similar label on a tall round bottle which is also very fine but not quite so highly regarded as the earlier versions.

Three casks in particular have acquired an incredible reputation: 441, 442 and 443. They were sherry casks and each was bottled separately at cask strength at a mere 24 years of age. They exhibit a depth and intensity of flavour that has left experienced tasters breathless and are, for the enthusiastic Springbank drinker, as close to perfection as it is possible to come.

Springbank was closed for most of the 1980s, restarting fully in 1989. The quality of some of the early production from that period has been criticised as erratic but that seems to have worked through the system and its reputation is growing again. It's a huge challenge for the present team, though, to produce something as remarkable as these whiskies. The quality and availability of modern sherry casks represents a challenge – perhaps these are whiskies that can never again be reproduced, in which case those few fortunate individuals who were able to acquire a bottle on the initial release at very modest prices can consider themselves blessed!

Once upon a time you could purchase a cask of new make and keep it all for yourself (and friends). Sadly, they don't offer that facility any longer, so even Springbank has been infected by progress.

I am not the biggest fan of marks out of 100, as you may have noticed, but cask 443 was awarded 96 points by Malt Maniacs, Serge Valentin and Olivier Humbrecht.

Put another way, that means it is very, very good. Some would say it's even better than that.

83

Producer
Distillery
Visitor Centre
Availability

Diageo
Stitzel-Weller, Louisville, USA
No
Limited specialists

Stitzel-Weller

Like many American distillery stories this one is complicated, featuring changes of ownership, the impact of Prohibition and the inevitable confusion of brand and distillery names. But, even though the distillery is closed, it has a hugely important place in the history of bourbon and many knowledgeable critics maintain that, in its day, Stitzel-Weller made the finest whiskey ever produced. So how come it lies cold and silent?

I saw it summed up very well on a website*: 'In its way, the old Stitzel-Weller Distillery is the perfect summation of distilling in Louisville: dormant, confusing, derelict, exploited, abandoned, proud, and promising.'

In short, the distillery was founded after the repeal of Prohibition by distinguished distilling families (Stitzel and Weller) and opened in 1935. They were soon making distinctive wheated bourbons that gained a very high reputation (although, as is the way of these things, that reputation appears to have grown since the distillery was closed and stocks began to run out).

Its heyday was under the ownership of the Van Winkle family but the decline in bourbon sales in the 1960s and 70s led them to sell out. The new owners fared little better and eventually the distillery passed into the hands of Guinness in 1986 and thence to Diageo, who closed it in 1992.

However, rights to the Pappy van Winkle brand remained with the family and, having hung on to some casks when they sold the distillery, they were able to continue bottling from the Stitzel-Weller stock. Today only the very oldest 23 Year Old comes from those stocks.

Confusing, isn't it? Unfortunately, it gets more so, because today Diageo uses the site of the Stitzel-Weller Distillery for its Bulleit Bourbon Experience, though that brand is distilled by Four Roses in Lawrenceburg. That's not untypical of the smoke and mirrors marketing that characterises much American whiskey, hence the cynicism apparent in the quote from the website above.

And it gets worse! Or possibly better, as, in the latest twist, Diageo sources have let slip that the distillery may be renovated and reopened. Previously the cost of removing asbestos from the plant was cited as being prohibitive and the reason that it would remain closed. If the stories are true then, presumably, the worldwide boom in demand means it's now viable. If so, hurrah! It won't be – it can't be – the same but it's great news in any event for a distillery that is a legend in its own right.

* See http://teleport-city.com/2013/01/02/urban-bourbon-stitzel-weller/

84

Producer
Distillery
Visitor Centre
Availability

Lost

Alexander and MacDonald Ltd
Stronachie, Perth and Kinross
No
Auctions

Stronachie

Now you see it, now you don't.

Stronachie is a salutary reminder than Scotch whisky hasn't always been a licence to print money. In the middle of the current 'golden age' it might be prudent to recall the short and not particularly distinguished history of Stronachie. Think of this as the slave carrying the victorious Roman general's triumphant laurel wreath but offering reminders of mortality.

Stronachie lasted less than 40 years. Built in 1890 near the small town of Forgandenny in rural Perthshire under the ownership of Alexander MacDonald, in 1907 it was sold to Sir James Calder. All might have been well, as he was widely experienced in the industry, but greater economic forces were at work.

In 1920 it was absorbed into MacDonald, Greenlees of Leith, along with the Bo'ness distillery, and six years later it was acquired by The Distillers Company, along with Bo'ness, Auchinblae, Glendullan and Dalwhinnie. Of these five distilleries, only two remain open, though pedants would immediately observe that the original Glendullan has been replaced by a new distillery of the same name*.

Stronachie was closed almost immediately, dismantled and the site cleared by 1930. All that remains are a few stone walls, the odd water jug that appears on auction sites and, allegedly, four bottles in private collections§.

The plot thickens, though, as in 2002 bottles of a smartly packaged Stronachie, billed as being from 'the lost distillery' started to appear on shelves. Had some casks miraculously survived? Sadly, the truth is rather more banal. Based on the fact that independent bottler A D Rattray had been the sales agents for Stronachie in an earlier incarnation (80 years previously, mind you), they launched what they suggested was malt whisky recreating the style and flavours of this lost distillery and named it thus.

In fact, it was from Benrinnes which, in due course, new legislation required them to make clear on the label, thus rather defeating the 'mystery malt' angle. This was, of course, part of the point of the legislation: that consumers should know exactly what they are buying and not be seduced, however briefly, by the idea that they have found something extraordinarily rare and precious.

There is no need for any mystery. You can buy various expressions of Benrinnes and a perfectly sound drop it is, too. As for Stronachie, well that really is lost and I doubt if anyone will ever taste it again.

* And, what's more, they'd be right. Damn their eyes.
§ One may be seen on display at the A D Rattray Whisky Experience in Kirkoswald, Ayrshire.

85

Producer
Distillery
Visitor Centre
Availability

Diageo
Talisker, Isle of Skye
Yes
Widespread

www.malts.com

Talisker Storm

'There is not,' declared owner John Anderson in 1878, 'a whisky gets a better reputation on the market or brings a better price than Talisker whisky.' Shortly afterwards he went bust.

Seven years later, in his poem 'The Scotsman's Return From Abroad', Robert Louis Stevenson eulogised it as 'The king o' drinks, as I conceive it'; though, in strict fairness he did go on to mention 'Islay or Glenlivet' as well. Rather strangely, he included this endorsement in a collection of verse for children, which I can't imagine would be very well received these days.

The distillery is famously the only one on the island of Skye, which always seems peculiar to me. One might have expected a more vibrant distilling tradition there. Back in 1823 there were seven distilleries recorded: perhaps other distillers, having tasted Talisker, simply gave up.

Whatever the reason, the forceful single malt from this fiercely traditional distillery is greatly loved. It has been sold as a single malt for many years, though the purist might mention that it was triple distilled until 1928 so the whisky drunk by Stevenson would have tasted rather different to the 'lava of the Cuillins' that we get today.

I'm sure that there are legends associated with Talisker and Skye (the usual cheesy faux-Gaelic stuff run up to impress the tour bus market and promptly forgotten) but for me one unforgettable moment was watching legendary BBC TV weatherman Michael Fish get thoroughly drenched on London's South Bank in order to promote – you've guessed it – Talisker Storm. I assume he was handsomely remunerated but also showed himself a sporting gentleman.

This may not mean very much to you if you're reading this outside the UK or if you're much under 30, in which case you should immediately consult YouTube. Fish is renowned for his famous on-air dismissal of the October 1987 extratropical cyclone that caused such damage in the south of England. Mind you, it was rated little more than a summer breeze on Skye.

Anyway, back to the whisky. If you haven't tried it, you should. If you have, you'll know why.

It is, I'll admit, an acquired taste and not everyone will enjoy this peaty, punchy, pungent potion. But if you do, you do. Unaged it may be, but Talisker Storm doesn't lack maturity. As a very pleasant alternative, Port Ruighe (Portree for the Sassenachs) is a port-finished version in more limited distribution but is well worth the effort to track down.

Legend

Unknown
Any
Read the book
Perhaps best avoided

The Demon Whisky

What's this? The Demon Whisky? Well, I believe that we should neither forget nor underestimate the influence of the Temperance and Prohibition movements. The legend of whisky as a category has been defined as much by its opponents as its enthusiasts.

Lurid images of drunken debauchery, criminality, disease and degradation were a vivid part of their campaigning. In the early 19th century tracts such as George B. Cheever's *The Dream: or, The True Story of Deacon Giles' Distillery* (1835) were reprinted numerous times, presumably because Temperance reformers found them effective. The social evils of excessive consumption of cheap distilled spirits were obvious to reformers and a source of great misery, particularly among the unemployed and working classes. However, no one social group is immune to such problems and the literature frequently features respectable members of society who fell from grace due to the demon drink.

That phrase – the demon drink – has thus passed into the language. The illustration is taken from Charles Mackay's *The Whisky Demon; or, The Dream of the Reveller*, published in Edinburgh in 1860. Vividly illustrated* by Watts Phillips, the poem dramatically foretells the fate of the reveller – doomed to end his days of carousing in one of the Demon's three houses: jail, the workhouse or a lazar house§ ('Rank, fetid, and unholy').

The illustration shows the Whisky Demon riding over his unfortunate followers who are seen brawling, abandoning their children and crying desperately for just one more drop from the cask of whisky he carries. Today we may treat such imagery as a source of amusement and scoff at the Victorian melodrama of much Temperance literature. But when we remember the scourge of cheap alcohol, and today's continued problems of alcohol abuse, the joke somewhat sours. Perhaps the proponents of minimum unit pricing for alcohol are the spiritual successors to the Temperance movement? They certainly claim the same moral authority.

Much cheap 'whisky' was heavily adulterated with all kinds of remarkable additives; some, such as meths, shellac gum, sulphuric acid and boot polish, were quite capable all-too-literally of 'finishing off' the unfortunates who consumed itº.

The 'Demon' was a very real part of many lives.

* Such illustrations were often employed as 'magic lantern' slides in Temperance lectures, along with vivid personal testimony from reformed alcoholics who had taken the pledge.

§ I trust you haven't forgotten: this was where poor unfortunates suffering from leprosy ended up.

º See Edward Burns, *Bad Whisky*, NWP Glasgow, if you don't believe me.

87

Producer
Distillery
Visitor Centre
Availability

Chivas Brothers Ltd
The Glenlivet, Ballindalloch, Morayshi
Yes
Widespread

www.theglenlivet.com

The Glenlivet
18 Years Old

'The human mind never tires o'Glenlivet, any mair than o'caller [fresh] air. If a body could just find oot the exac' proper proportion and quantity that ought to be drunk every day, and keep to that, I verily trow [swear] that he might leeve forever, without dying at a', and that doctors and kirk-yards would go oot o'fashion.'

That at any rate was the opinion of the autodidact James Hogg, 'the Ettrick Shepherd', poet, novelist and, according to Wordsworth, 'a man of original genius, but of coarse manners and low and offensive opinions.' So, well qualified as a whisky writer, then. However, he probably didn't mean The Glenlivet specifically (not that it was styled as such then anyway) but this one brand has come to stand for the whole region.

George IV is said to have asked for Glenlivet on his grand procession through Edinburgh in 1822, though with no very great discrimination (he was also partial to cherry brandy). The fact of his cheerfully consuming in public bumpers of what was still very much an illegal, smuggled product had a profound influence on the fortunes of Scotch whisky, though. Indeed, it may have contributed to the political climate in which the radical reforms of the 1823 Excise Act (itself a legendary piece of legislation in terms of whisky) were possible.

Such was the reputation of the Glen of the Livet that for many years it was sardonically referred to as 'the longest glen in Scotland'*. Though the owners of the eponymous distillery obtained a court judgment entitling them to use the definitive article, other distillers were permitted to hyphenate their name to that of the region, which they did with gusto – an early example of parasite marketing!

In recent years The Glenlivet has been greatly expanded by its present owners, who have heavily promoted the brand, laying great emphasis on its rich heritage and history, which are indeed central to the legends and romance of Scotch whisky. 'The single malt that started it all', they like to assert – and no one has convincingly refuted that claim, though there is a whiff of the copywriter about it.

Personally, I don't think I would tire of the distillery's fine 18 Years Old version. It's not hard to track down and well worth the effort.

There's hardly room here to mention the original founder's habit of carrying a pair of pistols (out of necessity, mind you, for self-defence), nor Sir Walter Scott's verdict in *St Ronan's Well* that Glenlivet is 'the only liquor fit for a gentleman to drink in the morning.'

Let the Wizard of the North[§] have the last word: 'It is worth all the wines of France for flavour, and more cordial to the system besides.'

* The longest is actually Glen Lyon. Not that I have measured it.
[§] Old Sir Walter himself.

88

Producer
Distillery
Visitor Centre
Availability

The Last Drop Distillers Ltd
n/a – this is a blend
No
Specialists

Luxurious

www.lastdropdistillers.com

The Last Drop

A curious story this, and something of a last hurrah by three veterans of the drinks industry, Tom Jago, James Espey, and Peter Fleck, who between them have over 120 years in the Scotch industry. With luck and a great deal of hard work, they will make a huge success of this, create an alluring premium brand and be bought out at enormous profit to enjoy a well-earned retirement!

Looking to do something very different and exclusive in whisky, they set off on a search. After a bit of digging, they found three very unusual casks of whisky at Auchentoshan Distillery, near Glasgow. Strange, orphaned casks like these do turn up from time to time, throwing up extraordinary, wonderful and unexpected results. In this case, they contained whisky distilled no later than 1960 (exact details of provenance are vague), which had been married together in 1972 and then basically forgotten for the next 36 years until the Last Drop team stumbled across them.

As you might expect, the angels had done their work and all that remained when the casks were opened was a mere 1,347 bottles. So they didn't mess about. No dilution from cask strength (a remarkable 52%) and no chill filtration. It went into a simple box, with a nice booklet and a mini. An elegant, tasteful and distinguished presentation that didn't rely on ritzy packaging to tell the story.

And, of course, it sold out.

Despite their combined age, the team remain active and have also launched a 60-year-old Cognac (478 bottles), which also sold out. Quite soon there will be a Last Drop single malt and a 50-year-old blended whisky (388 bottles).

With these products you get something remarkable: access to many, many years of knowledge and experience (these fellows would never put their name to anything short of excellent) and some of the last of the 'lost casks' that have turned up in odd corners of dusty warehouses. With greatly improved and more sophisticated stock control, and with sales and marketing folks taking a greater interest in super-premium, niche products, there aren't going to be many more of these. So enjoy them while you can.

If you look hard you might find some in a duty free shop somewhere, in which case, if you like old blends and rich deep flavours you should snap it up.

89

Producer
Distillery
Visitor Centre
Availability

Loch Fyne Whiskies
n/a – this is a blend
Shop in Inveraray, Argyll and Bute
As above and online

www.lfw.co.uk

The Living Cask

Back in July 1920 the noted literary critic and oenophile Professor George Saintsbury published his *Notes on a Cellar-Book*. In those war-weary days it was an immediate success, being reprinted four times by 1923. Such is its reputation and influence that it remains in print to this day and second-hand copies are easily and cheaply to be found. His is a name to inspire respect among drinks writers; a legend in his own right.

He devoted a scant eight pages to whisky. But what pages! In them we find his trenchant views ('I had never cared, and do not to this day care, much for the advertised blends, which, for this or that reason the public likes, or thinks it likes.') and the following magnificently impractical recommendation:

'The more excellent way [to store whisky at home]… is to establish a cask of whatever size your purse and cellar will admit, from a butt to an "octave" (14 gallons), or an "anker" (ten), or even less; fill it up with good and drinkable whisky from six to eight years old, stand it up on end, tap it half-way down or even a little higher and, when you get to or near the tap, fill it up again with whisky fit to drink, but not too old.'

What a splendid proposition, and what a splendid prospect such a cask would present. But, it must be admitted, hardly a realistic one in today's home. Even if your partner would agree.

There is a solution. Inspired by Professor George Saintsbury, the inimitable Richard Joynson*, then proprietor of Loch Fyne Whiskies in Inveraray, launched his Living Cask.

Adorned by the illustration of the 'cask boy' from Aeneas MacDonald's poetic little book *Whisky*, the Loch Fyne Living Cask follows Saintsbury's recommendation to the letter. Once upon a time it was available as an entirely indulgent full bottle, but is normally sold in quantities of 20cl. Naturally, it changes constantly as the whiskies added to the cask vary over time.

Despite Loch Fyne Whiskies having recently been sold to a national chain of whisky specialists, they have confirmed to me that the Living Cask will live on. So, in effect, we get a delightfully subtle reference to three legends for the price of one: Saintsbury devised this, Richard Joynson brought it into modern cellars, and Aeneas MacDonald's 'cask boy' graces the label[§].

It tastes good as well.

* According to the normally reliable Charles MacLean, Joynson was 'once a fish'. I have my doubts about this.

[§] Interesting bonus fact – MacDonald knew Saintsbury, attending his lectures at Edinburgh University shortly after the Great War.

90

Producer
Distillery
Visitor Centre
Availability

The Macallan Distillers
Macallan, Craigellacchie, Morayshi
Yes
Auctions and specialists

www.themacallan.com

The Macallan 1928

Over 50 Years Old

You will notice quite a few entries for The Macallan here. This is the first of six, in fact (I checked). That is because The Macallan is The Daddy, as far as legendary whiskies go*.

Today it's a luxury brand that thinks nothing of charging £10,000+ for its new releases and is able to spend £100 million (yes, £100 million, not a typo) on its new distillery and visitor centre, while at the same time having the long-term goal of reaching the one million case sales mark and then aiming to overhaul the global single malt category leader Glenfiddich. So it seems that it has attained a remarkable position of being all things to all men, while retaining incredible desirability and lustre.

But it didn't start out quite like that. Not so very long ago, The Macallan sold even its oldest whiskies at prices which most lovers of single malt could afford. Take this incredible Over 50 Years Old release[§]: it was originally sold in the UK, Germany, France and the USA for around £50 but, as its reputation grew, the price steadily increased. Admittedly this was in 1983 but, applying the RPI index to that, it suggests an equivalent price in 2012 of £143. I'd take a few bottles for that.

With only 500 bottles released and, presumably, a considerable number of them enjoyed, this legendary whisky is now extremely difficult to find. As they say at The Whisky Exchange (where they will sell you one of the remaining few bottles for £30,000): 'A bona fide treasure for collectors, the release of The Macallan 1928 50yo was a major landmark for one of the world's most famous distilleries and remains a key event in the history of single malt whisky itself.'

And that's why this particular bottle is here. Six entries may seem overkill (their rivals will certainly think so) but they go to demonstrate that The Macallan has been creating legends consistently for more than 30 years and is very much the trendsetter in this field. It will be fascinating to see if they can go on for another three decades.

Incidentally, they couldn't do this now. This was bottled at its natural cask strength of 38.6%, well below the 40% standard which is now the legal minimum bottling strength for all whiskies. So, taking a purist line, I have decided not to taste it.

You can believe that if you like.

* Though, to be fair, Bowmore comes close. The Macallan achieves higher prices at auction; although, again, Bowmore has had its successes.

[§] It was actually 55 years old. Today it would be packaged in Lalique crystal.

199

91

Producer
Distillery
Visitor Centre
Availability

Luxurious

The Macallan Distillers
Macallan, Craigellacchie, Morayshi
Yes
Very limited

The Macallan 1938

I'm probably going to run out of things to tell you about The Macallan. That's the problem with legends, there are only so many superlatives in the dictionary.

But this is an interesting bottling, effectively the beginning of 'modern' The Macallan and it marks an evolution on their pathway to legendary status. In 1938 The Macallan was – like virtually every other distillery in Scotland – producing exclusively for the blending market. Still being independently owned in those days and not having a blended brand of their own, the distillery relied on sales to brokers and to other distillers who did market a blend. So, if they weren't careful they could produce too much or too little whisky in any given season, which would leave them with a problem.

That's another thing to note: back then, before WW2, distillers thought in terms of 'seasons'. The summer 'silent season' was longer and distilling was more intimately connected to agricultural rhythms than it is today. So something obviously happened around 1938* which meant that years later the distillery was carrying unusually large stocks of this vintage.

And here's something else to note: the current fashion for very old whiskies is quite a recent one. When The Macallan first released a 25-year-old they were pretty much on their own. There was (it was thought) very little demand for it so very little was produced (even assuming there was any available). As a result, very little was sold, leading the distillers to conclude that they had been right all along and that there really was very little demand. It wasn't until the stocks of the great whisky loch§ started to be released in the 1990s that much interest was created. A new generation of sales and marketing executives realised that they could not only sell this old whisky, but they could get very fancy prices for it. And so we find ourselves where we are today.

So this modestly adorned bottle of The Macallan, released in 1980 to mark the appointment of distributors as far afield as Scotland, France, Australia and New Zealand proved quite visionary.

Little did anyone anticipate that this was the harbinger of whiskies at £15,000 and more for a single bottle. The folks who released this would be astonished and possibly a little shocked by what they started. And, great whisky though this is, I'm not entirely sure we should thank them.

* Some trouble with Herr Hitler, I understand.
§ A term coined to describe the excess stocks that accumulated prior to the draconian cuts and closures of the early 1980s.

92

Producer
Distillery
Visitor Centre
Availability

The Macallan Distillers
Macallan, Craigellacchie, Morayshi
Yes
Auctions

The Macallan 1926
60 Years Old Peter Blake

Once upon a time – a near-legendary period, now lost in the mists of time – when The Macallan was still an independent company, it was run by creative souls who did strange and unexpected things that the rest of the whisky industry regarded as dangerously quixotic.

Typical of such eccentric behaviour was the decision in 1986 to release just 12 bottles of 60-year-old whisky in individually labelled bottles, with a label design by the noted British father of pop art Sir Peter Blake.

For a while, nothing much happened. Then, in 1991, to general disbelief, a Japanese collector and bar owner paid the astonishing, breathtaking, outrageous sum of £6,250 for a bottle at Christie's. Hard though it may be to believe, this was then the world-record price for a bottle of whisky. Something very important to whisky happened that day.

Buoyed by this success, they repeated the exercise in 1993, this time with labels by Italian artist Valerio Adami, and beat their own auction world record when a bottle sold in London in aid of a licensed trade charity for £12,100 in 1996. Gasps all round. Note, please, how long it took to release just 12 bottles to the market: this was a carefully stage-managed exercise that has created the platform for The Macallan to be the most sought-after whisky in the world today*.

At the time these whiskies were released the general view was scepticism. Few people believed that whisky could command this sort of price but those who believed it was justified and acted on that view have been richly rewarded. I would not care to speculate on what a bottle of The Macallan Blake would fetch today at auction.

Actually, yes I will. It would have to be six figures, possibly a quarter of a million pounds or more. When you consider that the record price for a Blake original, his *Loelia, World's Most Tattooed Lady*, is £337,250 (Christie's November 2010), that is an extraordinary amount.

Rather charmingly Blake's connection with The Macallan was celebrated in June 2012 with the release of just 250 examples of a piece named *The Macallan and Sir Peter Blake Celebrate Eight Decades*. This consisted of an oak box, divided into eight sections, each decade having a backdrop and artefact designed, inspired or chosen by Sir Peter Blake; a miniature of The Macallan distilled in the relevant decade with labels designed by Sir Peter and a small book of illustrations and text about his life.

Launched with the price of £4,500, all were gone in days and have already risen substantially in value. Changed days.

93

Luxurious

Producer	Highland Distillers Ltd
Distillery	Macallan, Craigellacchie, Morayshire
Visitor Centre	Yes
Availability	One only

www.themacallan.com

The Macallan

Cire Perdue

These special releases can be rather vulgar sometimes. In their eagerness to ingratiate themselves with the filthy rich who buy such things, the distillers are occasionally guilty of overdoing the packaging – of gilding the lily, one might say.

I don't care for all of The Macallan's releases in Lalique crystal, though that is a matter of taste and aesthetics. I don't suppose for a moment that either Lalique or The Macallan or even their filthy rich customers have the slightest interest in my opinion. However, just in case they are concerned, I'll say that I believe this particular expression to be a thing of elegance and grace.

There's only one of them, however. It was created using the ancient 'cire perdue', or lost wax, process that Lalique has not employed since 1930 and, in the flesh, it is strikingly beautiful. It was filled with 64 Years Old The Macallan single malt and then taken on a world tour to raise money for the Charity: water campaign. When you consider the amount of water used to make crystal and indeed whisky, and the pressing need for clean and safe water in the developing world, there could hardly be a more fitting partnership. Impressively, every penny – not just the profit – was donated to the charity.

The twelve-city road show and auction raised a total of $604,105. The tight-fisted Parisians gave least ($5,000) and the good people of Hong Kong the most ($17,470), with the auction hammer falling at $460,000* at Sotheby's New York on 15th November 2010. I regard this all as very commendable. Lalique and The Macallan got lots of publicity, and I suppose they managed to sell some of their less expensive items off the back of it. But that seems fair enough for such a worthy and important cause.

This design was a one-off but, should you want your own Lalique decanter filled with rare and old whisky, The Macallan do release these annually, generally around the £15,000 mark. I'm told that people do drink the whisky. I have no idea what they do with their empties, though I am fairly certain they don't end up in the recycling bin.

Generally speaking, very old The Macallans are rich, elegant and complex. Ironically, in this case, they don't really need or want any added water.

Or, so I have been told.

* If that seems like a lot of money, it's because it is. But then, it was a very large decanter.

94

Producer
Distillery
Visitor Centre
Availability

The Macallan Distillers
Macallan, Craigellacchie, Morayshire
Yes
Auctions and specialists

The Macallan
Replica Series

This is a curious and tangled story. Perhaps only The Macallan could have got away with creating 'replicas' of 19th-century whiskies based on a series of fakes. Well, all but one of them were fakes. And I suppose our story starts with this genuine article.

In 1996 (just prior to The Macallan being owned by Highland Distillers Ltd), the first Macallan Replica was launched. This was a modern whisky created by Frank Newlands, then the company's Whisky Maker, which aimed to recreate the nose and taste of an 1874 bottle that the company had bought at auction for £4,000.

Most commentators now agree that this bottle and the whisky in it were genuine and that the replica was a pretty decent approximation of the original, if a little less delicate. It was launched at £75 for a bottle and performed well.

The Macallan, perhaps without being fully conscious of the fact, was on its way to becoming a positional good*. The new owners, impressed by the idea of selling 12,000 bottles at such premium prices followed this up with further replicas: 1861 (2001); 1841 (2002); 1876 (2003); and the 1851 Inspiration (not strictly part of the Replica Series) in 2004, though it was available only in the Far East.

Pretty soon, however, the Replica Series turned into an embarrassment, as it became clear that all the later bottles had been based on elaborately constructed fakes purchased by the company. They had, in fact, been duped. But they were not alone – there was a wave of highly suspicious old bottles appearing on otherwise reputable auction sites and seducing collectors. The writer Dave Broom did great work in exposing the counterfeit trade and The Macallan lost a lot of credibility with the more knowledgeable whisky enthusiasts and collectors.

But with The Macallan's global appeal outstripping the influence of such old guard whisky commentators, the controversy appears to have had little or no long-term influence on the brand's fortunes. However, the Replica Series was quietly dropped (rumour has it that the 1851 Inspiration was to have been the fifth but was repackaged to avoid the by-now tainted association) and the display of 'original' bottles proudly shown in the visitor centre was discreetly removed.

The Replica Series is finished and quietly forgotten but, in the final irony, collectors now buy the Replicas as amusing facsimiles of fakes!

* See Fred Hirsch, *The Social Limits to Growth*. A 'positional good' is a product whose value is at least in part a function of its ranking in desirability by others.

95

Producer Highland Distillers Ltd
Distillery Macallan, Craigellacchie, Morayshi[re]
Visitor Centre Yes
Availability One only

Luxurious

The Macallan
M Constantine Decanter

If you have just read the entry for The Macallan Peter Blake bottles you may have formed the conclusion that I feel the brand's best days of innovation are behind it; now that it is in corporate ownership, not private hands, it has all got rather safe and predictable; run, in fact, by accountants, not artists.

And, truth to tell, a few years ago I might have argued that to be the case. Not now: lately, it seems to me that The Macallan has got at least some of its edgy, radical spirit back. They are starting to do some quite unusual and striking things that echo the bold experiments of the previous owners.

Very few whiskies, for example, would hire the fashion photographer Rankin and release a limited run of 1,000 bottles, each with a completely different label, many of which featured a naked lady draped over the stills or casks of whisky. It could have been dreadfully reminiscent of page 3 of *The Sun*, but the images were (just) the right side of soft porn. The Macallan was exposed to a new audience*.

Or take this decanter of The Macallan M. M is Macallan's latest, non-aged, luxury offering – £3,000 for the standard bottle, sorry *decanter*, a hard-edged modern design which is anything but traditional (though I suppose if you squint a bit it resembles The Antiquary). It's made, of course, by Lalique; designed by Fabien Baron, renowned for his work in fashion, cosmetics and other high-end luxury goods; and contains a 44.7% abv whisky, said to contain some spirit dating back to the 1940s.

That's all very nice, but not all that remarkable. However, possessed by the original Macallan spirit of adventure, they went on to create with Lalique four six-litre Imperiale decanters; the largest ever made by the French crystal house. Each took more than 50 hours of highly skilled work to complete. They stand over 70cm tall and weigh nearly 17kg once full (hard to imagine they'll ever be empty, so they'll need a big shelf).

Of the four, two will be archived by The Macallan and one has been committed to a private collector in Asia. The fourth, *Constantine* (named, as are the others, after Roman emperors), was sold by Sotheby's in Hong Kong for a staggering US$628,000 (£381,620) – another world record, of course.

I think that's probably enough Macallan now.

96

Producer
Distillery

Visitor Centre
Availability

The Number One Drinks Company
Karuizawa Distillery, Kitasakugun,
Nagano, Japan
No – the distillery has been demolished
A few specialists – while stocks last

www.one-drinks.com

The Number One Drinks Company

Can't afford The Number One Drinks Company's Karuizawa 1964 (see earlier entry)? Well, the 1976 is a single-cask bottling (63% abv) from their 'Noh' series (hence the very striking label, which features a traditionally dressed performer from classical Noh theatre, one of Japan's great cultural treasures).

Whiskies are sourced in Japan by the co-owner David Croll; samples are assessed by a tasting panel prior to selection; casks are then purchased, bottled and shipped to the UK and a few European stockists to be sold to specialist retailers and trendier pubs and bars. All this means they can be hard to find, bottles are often pre-ordered by the well-informed and, accordingly, they sell out very quickly, even at quite high prices. In short, you have to get in quick if you want any.

But it's well worth making the effort. I've picked just one of their expressions, current at time of going to print, as an example but you can be pretty confident of anything you track down with their label.

Make a note of those labels, as well – The Number One Drinks Company make a point of handsome packaging, which just adds to the aesthetic experience.

You might, if you're very lucky, find something from Hanyu bottled by them. The Karuizawa distillery was closed in 2000 but a new owner Ichiro Akuto, the grandson of the founder, established a company called Venture Whisky to produce single malt whisky and has established a new whisky distillery at Chichibu. The Hanyu expressions are now rare, highly desirable and among the most interesting whiskies from a more-than-interesting producer nation. Akuto-san's Chichibu products are now also available from Number One Drinks.

Essentially, this is a boutique operation run part-time by the owners, which is part of the increasing diversity, interest and excitement of the world of whisky. Their enthusiasm, detailed knowledge and ability to source really obscure but high-quality drams mark them out as a business to follow with interest. Just don't expect any bargains as they are well aware of the value and global interest in their releases.

Just so that we are clear about this, I will say it again: get in quick. You snooze, you lose!

That's how legends roll.

97

Luxurious

Producer	Angus Dundee Distillers plc
Distillery	Tomintoul, Morayshire
Visitor Centre	Last seen in McTears Auction room, Glasgow
Availability	Apparently still available

www.worldslargestscotchwhisky.com

Tomintoul 14

The eagle-eyed whisky enthusiasts among you will no doubt be reeling backwards with shock at this point. 'What,' you are asking in tones of horror, 'is Tomintoul 14 doing in here? That's not a legendary whisky,' you scream at the page. 'Has Buxton lost his mind?'

It's a perfectly acceptable wee whisky, of course, from a relatively modern distillery close to the village of Tomintoul, the highest village in the Highlands (this is completely irrelevant, by the way). Known as 'the gentle dram' you can pick up a bottle for around £35 – quite the bargain, in fact; although, as the description makes clear, this is not some roaring, peat-soaked, sherry-drenched monster. Perhaps it's a little too self-effacing for its own good. 'After you, Angus,' it seems to say, and other whiskies elbow it out of the way.

But one day in January 2009, distraught at the prospect that Sir Terry Wogan would no longer be mentioning Tomintoul on his breakfast radio show*, local restaurateur Dru McPherson convinced Mike and Cathy Drury of The Whisky Castle shop that what Tomintoul needed was the world's largest bottle of whisky. It's obvious when you come to think about it. So – to cut a long story short – they had a huge 105-litre bottle and massive cork made and filled it with the equivalent of 150 standard bottles of 14-year-old Tomintoul single malt. A local MP turned out to unveil the bottle, which was subsequently ratified by Guinness World Records as 'The Largest Bottle of Scotch Whisky in the World'. Hold me back.

Enormous crowds of tourists then flocked to Tomintoul to witness this miracle and to be permitted to kiss the bottle. Tragically, a group of German single malt whisky enthusiasts were crushed to death in the pandemonium that followed. [*Are you sure about this? Ed§*.]

In October 2012 it went on display in the Scotch Whisky Heritage Centre in Edinburgh. After a period of public exhibition it was consigned to McTears of Glasgow, the auctioneers, and offered for sale in December 2013 with an estimate of between £100,000 and £150,000.

Er, unfortunately, it didn't sell. In a masterly display of understatement, McTears' Steven McGinty commented, 'Today just wasn't the day when someone felt inclined to bid for it.'

It would appear that you can't just manufacture a legendary whisky.

* Give the man a break. He was 71, for goodness' sake.
§ On second thoughts, I may have imagined this. It should have happened, though.

98

Producer

Distillery

Visitor Centre

Availability

A number of different companies ha[...]
bottles on board

n/a – being pre-war the cargo
comprised blends

You could go to Barra and gaze at
the sea, I suppose

Possibly at auction

Whisky Galore!

The SS *Politician* was an 8,000-ton cargo ship owned by T & J Harrison Ltd of Liverpool. It left Liverpool on 3 February 1941, bound for Kingston, Jamaica, and New Orleans with a cargo including 28,000 cases of whisky. The ship sank near the island of Eriskay in the Outer Hebrides, off the west coast of Scotland, where much of the wreck's cargo was salvaged (or 'looted' depending on your point of view) by the islanders. The story of the wreck, the recovery of the whisky and the subsequent efforts of the authorities to recover the cargo (there were also banknotes on board) was the basis for Compton Mackenzie's book (1947) and the well-loved Ealing Studios film *Whisky Galore!*

So much is fact. However, despite the cloud of romance surrounding the islanders' 'liberation' of the whisky, no one knows with any certainty how much whisky was removed and how much remained when the *Politician* was eventually dynamited.

We can be pretty certain, however, that virtually all of the whisky recovered was immediately drunk due to the exigencies of wartime – and thanks to the zeal of the authorities attempting to recover it, immediate consumption will have seemed the most appropriate option. Certainly, the idea of collecting whisky would have been a wholly alien and bewildering concept to a Hebridean islander more than 70 years ago.

However, salvage efforts in the 1980s recovered 32 bottles. The bottle illustrated was part of a parcel of eight sold in November 1987 by Donald MacPhee, a diver from South Uist, which raised £4,000 (or £500 each).

Two from that parcel of eight were auctioned in 2013 by Glasgow's Scotch Whisky Auctions, an online web auction house specialising in collectable bottles, with the determined buyer paying £12,050 (£13,225 after auctioneer's commission). So someone made a pretty penny.

Some recovered in a second salvage attempt were used to create an SS *Politician* blend, bottles of which fetch a couple of hundred pounds. They have never really excited collections.

These original bottles are the stuff of legend because the mythology of the Scots and their relationship with whisky owes a lot to Mackenzie's book. If you have never read it, do so without delay.

This is a whisky best enjoyed on the rocks (ho, ho, ho!). By the way, there may be a few bottles still hidden in the machair on Eriskay. Good luck!

99

Producer	The New Zealand Malt Whisky Company Ltd
Distillery	Willowbank, South Island, New Zealand
Visitor Centre	No
Availability	Specialists

www.thenzwhisky.com

Willowbank

Be honest. You didn't realise there was a New Zealand whisky – let alone a distilling industry on the far side of the world. You thought it was full of hobbits and sheep.

But, once upon a time, a modest industry did flourish there. Think about it for a moment and it's no surprise: masses of Scottish settlers, a landscape not dissimilar to their home country and a fledgling agricultural industry. What better to do during the long nights and lonely days than set up a still and remind yourself of home.

Sadly, it didn't exactly prosper. After a brief burst of activity in the 19th century, most operators went out of business. However, the Willowbank Distillery near Dunedin* ran from 1974 to 1997, when it was mothballed. In 2000, just as the current whisky boom was beginning its amazing long run, the then-owners (Fosters, the brewers) stripped out the stills and sent them to Fiji to make rum. Great timing.

At first, no one seemed to know what to do with the remaining casks, which have been bottled as Lammerlaw, Wilson and Milford. There is even a Water of Leith, named for the distillery which preceded Willowbank (was that really such a good omen, given its history?) and which proudly boasts of the 'pure waters' that went into the whisky. I assume they haven't visited Leith (a now-gentrified quarter of the city but with a less-than-salubrious original reputation) or seen the original Water of Leith, with its fine collection of shopping trolleys and used needles§.

Today you will find the remaining Willowbank whiskies marketed by The New Zealand Malt Whisky Company Ltd who have benefited from the growing interest in world whiskies. So visible has NZ whisky become that the New Zealand Doublewood release drew a 'cease and desist' letter from William Grant & Sons Distillers Ltd, owners of The Balvenie, alleging that it infringed their DoubleWood trademark. TNZMWC responded by offering a free miniature of The Balvenie with a bottle of their own to let buyers decide which they prefer. Good use of humour there.

You'll probably buy this more as a novelty and to confuse your mate who's a (self-proclaimed) whisky expert. It will.

* The second-largest city on NZ's South Island, named for *Dùn Èideann*, Scots Gaelic for Edinburgh and not, as one whisky 'journalist' would have you believe, a compound of Dundee and Edinburgh.
§ Note to City of Edinburgh Council: this is a joke. Last time I was there I enjoyed strolling on the very pleasant walkway along its near-sylvan banks of verdant green. OK?

100

Producer	Suntory
Distillery	Yamazaki, near Osaka, Honshu Island, Japan
Visitor Centre	Yes
Availability	Widespread

www.suntory.com

Yamazaki

12 Years Old

Yamazaki 12 Years Old was the first Japanese single malt of any international significance. Based on its success, the company has gone on to release a considerable range of single malts and blends (notably the multi-award-winning Hibiki).

But should Shinjiro Torii or Masataka Taketsuru be considered as the father of Japanese whisky? Both have their claims, though Taketsuru is probably the stronger candidate. There had been earlier attempts to manufacture whisky in Japan but Taketsuru travelled to Scotland in 1918, studied briefly in Glasgow and obtained practical experience at Longmorn, Bo'ness and Hazelburn distilleries before returning home. It had been intended that he would start a Scotch-whisky-style distillery in Japan but these plans failed to materialise and he joined Shinjiro Torii in 1922.

Torii had prospered during WW1 and was equally determined to produce a high-quality whisky, so hired Taketsuru on generous terms with the aim of establishing a distillery on the Scottish model. This was opened at Yamazaki in November 1924 and is generally considered the first Japanese whisky distillery – perhaps predictably, Suntory tend to credit Torii with the choice of the site, while other commentators give the more experienced Taketsuru the credit. Today it is probably the best-known of the Japanese distilleries here in the West and its whiskies can be found in most specialists and even some supermarkets.

Together they launched the first recognised Japanese whisky, Shirofuda (White Label), but they parted company in 1934 when Taketsuru resigned to start his own operation at what became the Yoichi distillery. Today the two firms they created, Suntory and Nikka, are the dominant players in Japanese whisky.

Understandably, the firm's website tends to play down Masataka Taketsuru's role in the creation of Yamazaki and the birth of Japanese whisky, in favour of their own man Shinjiro Torii, but my feeling is that they deserve joint billing as whisky legends. Their creation, after a faltering start, has gone on to well-deserved international renown. Indeed Suntory have a powerful presence in Scotch whisky through their ownership of Morrison Bowmore (several of whose whiskies appear here) and they are a global force in whisky today.*

I think we can salute Yamazaki 12 Years Old as a legend in its own right and a symbol of Japanese whisky's new-found confidence.

* Having just bought Beam Inc. of the USA.

101

Producer
Distillery
Visitor Centre
Availability

Dionysos Bromios Blend*

'One day before we die,' Aeneas MacDonald writes in *Whisky*, 'some unknown fellow traveller in a railway compartment, some Scots ghillie or Irish rustic, may produce a flask or unlabelled bottle and we shall find ourselves at last in the presence of the god himself, Dionysos Bromios, God of Whisky.'

The name Aeneas MacDonald appeared in 1930, apparently out of nowhere, with *Whisky*, a slim, strangely poetic and passionate volume – and then disappeared, never to be heard again.

Or so it seemed. In fact, MacDonald was the pseudonym of George Malcolm Thomson, a prolific author and journalist who adopted this alias in deference to his mother's strictly teetotal preferences. *Whisky* is best seen as part of Thomson's fervent Scottish nationalism (his nom de plume was taken from one of Bonnie Prince Charlie's Seven Men of Moidart) and is important as the first work written about whisky from the point of view of the consumer. All the many whisky writers who have come after him, therefore, remain in his debt.

But it is no mere academic piece and remains fresh, absorbing and relevant. In an age of blends, Thomson prophetically championed the cause of 'self whiskies' and was sharply critical of the complacency of the industry and the indiscriminate manner in which much whisky was consumed. In declaring it worthy of as much care and consideration as fine wine, he was ahead of his time.

I urge, beseech and implore you to find a copy of *Whisky*, one of the finest and most profound things ever written about this tantalising subject and it is entirely fitting to leave the last word on legendary whiskies to his modest wee book.

The book concludes with reference to 'that romantic, unending quest of the true participator in the mysteries of aquavitae – the search for the perfect blend' and then, as MacDonald has it, 'we shall find ourselves at last in the presence of the god himself, Dionysos Bromios, God of Whisky.'

All lovers of whisky will recognise this as their ultimate goal, but will also recognise the quest itself as a journey that can never end. That is its frustration and its pleasure and why the ultimate legendary whisky – Aeneas MacDonald's perfect whisky; my perfect whisky; your perfect whisky – can only ever exist in legend, myth or the world of your imagination.

The End.

* Yes I know this is out of order alphabetically, but I wanted it to come last as it's the last word on legendary whiskies.

221

"By that Stowp! my faith an houpe,
And by
The dear
Kilbaigie"
CREAMY OLD
SCOTCH WHISKY
Thos. Stevenson,
Johnstone. N.B.

Acknowledgements

Along with Emma Tait and Darragh Deering of Headline, I dreamt up this book over a glass of Swiss whisky (yes, really). So it's their fault. Judy Moir eventually put the deal together with her customary imperturbable charm, tact and attention to detail.

Jo Roberts-Miller edited it and made me look good. Dr Nicholas Morgan, Christine McCafferty and the always cheerful Pat Roberts patiently helped out with my ever-more-obscure requests for information on Diageo brands and former distilleries; Bert Thomson guided me into the thicket which is the world of mini collectors; and, for many of the more hard-to-find illustrations, I turned to Jim and Linda Brown, whose collection of whisky ephemera is a constant source of wonder.

The Malt Maniacs website was a fount of whisky wisdom, and old copies of Michael Jackson's *Malt Whisky Companion* (from when Michael was still with us) were a very handy reference and companion.

Finally, very special thanks to the remarkable Sukhinder Singh of The Whisky Exchange whose knowledge, enthusiasm and authority was irreplaceable. Many of the illustrations were kindly provided by him or by his tireless colleague Michael Bryden. If you are ever in the fortunate position of being able to consider buying some of the whiskies here you could save yourself a lot of time and trouble by going straight to The Whisky Exchange's excellent website.

And, in the hope that I will eventually be forgiven, not forgetting Mrs Buxton who took charge of a major house move and subsequent renovations while I was writing most of this. Sorry about that.

Picture credits

The author and publisher acknowledge with thanks the following for supplying illustrations and photographs used in this book. All copyrights are acknowledged. Every effort has been made to fulfil requirements with regard to reproducing copyright material and the author and publisher will be glad to rectify any omissions or errors at the earliest opportunity.